Kathy Lamancusa's

❧ Guide to ❧

Wreath Making

TAB TAB BOOKS
Blue Ridge Summit, PA

Notices

Sahara II®	Smithers—Oasis Co.
Styrofoam®	Dow Chemical Corp.
Design Master®	Colorado Dye and Chemical Corp.
X-ACTO®	Hunt-Bienfang.

FIRST EDITION
FIRST PRINTING

© 1990 by Kathy Lamancusa
Published by TAB Books
TAB Books   is a division of McGraw-Hill, Inc.

Library of Congress Cataloging-in-Publication Data

Lamancusa, Kathy.
    [Guide to wreath making]
    Kathy Lamancusa's guide to wreath making / by Kathy Lamancusa.
       p.   cm.
    Includes index.
    ISBN 0-8306-6492-0   ISBN 0-8306-3492-4 (pbk.)
    1. Wreaths.   I. Title.
TT899.75.L36   1991
745.594'1—dc20   90-26978
                                                    CIP

TAB BOOKS offers software for sale. For information and a catalog, please contact TAB Software Department, Blue Ridge Summit, PA 17294-0850.

Questions regarding the content of this book should be addressed to:

   Reader Inquiry Branch
   TAB Books
   Blue Ridge Summit, PA 17294-0850

Acquisitions Editor: Kim Tabor
Book Editing and Design: Joanne M. Slike
Production: Katherine G. Brown
Page Makeup: Kimberly Shockey
Chapter-Opening Illustration: Jaclyn J. Boone
Cover Design: Lori E. Schlosser

Full page and cover photography by Shawn Wood, Studio 7, North Canton, OH

Contents

Chapter 3
Kitchen Wreaths 25

Chapter 4
Seasonal Wreaths 43

Chapter 5
Wreaths for Children 69

Chapter 6
Romantic Wreaths 79

✐ *Acknowledgments* ❧

I would like to thank the following people who assisted in making this book a reality:

My husband, Joe, who is always there when I need him and is ready, willing, and able to do whatever is necessary to keep our home and business running, while I bury myself in a manuscript.

My sons, Joey and Jimmy, who are patient, loving, and understanding every time I'm creating a book.

My mom, Stella Wielicki, whose handiwork I often utilize in my work.

My sister-in-law, Katherine Lamancusa, who is an extremely talented floral designer and designed some of the projects contained in this book.

My assistant, Mary Annette Salpietra, who assisted in the step-by-step hand shots and worked with me on the wreaths.

Further Acknowledgments:

Color and cover photography by Shawn Wood, Studio 7, North Canton, OH.

Wooden horse shown in top photo on page 6 of the color section designed and built by Casimir Wielicki.

Wood carving shown on page 7 of the color section by S. Joseph Lamancusa.

❧ Suppliers ☙

The following companies supplied products for use in the preparation of this book:

American Oak Preserving Co.
601 Mulberry St.
North Judson, IN 46366

B.B. World Corp.
2200 So. Maple Avenue
Los Angeles, CA 90011

Customfoam Crafts
1 Longfellow Place
Ludington, MI 49431

C.M. Offray & Son Inc.
Route 24   Box 601
Chester, N.J. 07903

Design Master Color Tool Inc.
P.O. Box 601
Boulder, CO 80306

Lion Ribbon Company
100 Metro Way
Secaucus, N.J. 07096

Loctite Corp.
4450 Cranwood Court
Cleveland, OH 44128

Lomey Manufacturing Corp.
P.O. Box 5314
Asheville, N.C. 28813

Rhyne Floral Supply
P.O. Box 310
Gastonia, N.C. 28053

Smithers—Oasis Co.
919 Marvin Avenue
Kent, OH 44240

Zucker Feather Products
512 North East Street
California, MO 65018

Introduction

Rich colors, beautiful textures, and combinations of materials can be used together to create truly spectacular wreaths and wallpieces for our own homes or the homes of our friends and loved ones.

I've written this book just for you—someone who loves to decorate with wreaths for any occasion. This book has been designed to give you enough wreath ideas so that you can change your wreaths as often as you like and still have plenty of ideas to spark your creativity when you're ready to make a new one.

The instructions are taught in an easy step-by-step format and many of the new concepts and techniques are illustrated with photographs that will carry you through each process without fail. Some of the designs might look complicated. Rest assured, all are quite easy to complete. Even if you have never made a wreath, you'll be able to follow these directions and achieve perfect results.

Whether you live in the United States or in another country, the materials for each project will be easy to find. In addition, I have included in parentheses metric equivalents for all measurements.

You might want to create an exact duplicate of the pictured project by carefully following instuctions, or you might want to experiment with the materials, making a wreath that is uniquely your own. Feel free to add or subtract elements of your choice. Simply keep the basic steps in mind as you create and adapt, using similar materials in the colors you wish to highlight.

The book is organized so that all preliminary instructions appear in the first two chapters. Chapter 1 explains the various types of materials and how they should be purchased, cut, and used. You will learn how to floral-tape, as well as how to take care of your wreaths after they are made.

Ribbon is the main focus of chapter 2. Bow making and creative ribbon techniques of all kinds are explained simply and clearly. In addition to learning how to make various types of bows, you will learn how to braid, shir, and create fans.

The remainder of the book is filled with dozens of easy-to-make projects, from whimsical to elegant. Each chapter focuses on a different theme. Wreaths for the kitchen are covered in chapter 3. Since we spend so much time in our kitchens, they are a great place to decorate. In chapter 3 you will learn how to preserve apples, cookies, and rolls. You will also learn how to incorporate interesting materials such as silk vegetables, wheat, garlic, peppers, and more to create truly memorable designs anyone would love to hang and admire.

Chapter 4 contains a multitude of wreaths designed for some of our most popular holidays, as well as a few to commemorate the seasons of the year. As our weather changes, so do our moods. We get anxious to decorate our homes to reflect these changes. An inexpensive way to do just that is to change the wreaths on our walls and doors. Several wreath designs are included to keep your home appropriately decorated all year-round. Holidays such as Halloween and Christmas are enthusiastically celebrated. We love to decorate and accent during these times.

The special world of children is depicted in the wreath designs in chapter 5, created for the young as well as the young at heart. The Ring of Hands wreath is designed specifically for children to make. Other designs are ideal for decorating children's rooms. You'll find the colors bright, cheery, and very inviting.

The wreaths in chapter 6 have the soft look of romantic styling. Pearls, feathers, lace, moiré, and satin are but a few of the elements incorporated in the designs. These wreaths can be used for feminine rooms or for the newly emerging decorating theme—Victorian.

It is a challenge to create wreath designs for men. Chapter 7 explains several options open to you. You'll use feathers, willow, grapevine, pods, and other "woodsy" materials. The wreath designs use colors that are dark and rich, making them perfect accents for dens, offices, libraries, or other rooms men occupy.

Chapter 8 presents a host of ideas for all those special occasions in our lives when we want to give someone a gift we've made ourselves. You'll find designs perfect for a house-warming, a baby shower, Mother's Day, or a birthday. I'm certain these ideas will spark others for you, too.

Stretch, reach, and grow. Use your instincts, along with the basic concepts presented here, to create designs you'll be proud to say you made. Show a little love and appreciation, or share a feeling with someone special by creating a spectacular wreath for them. Once it is hung in their homes, they will not soon forget you!

Relax and enjoy!!

Starting Out

Wreath making can be enjoyed by young and old alike. The round wreath is still the most popular. Perhaps because we learn to make a circle as one of our first shapes, we are most comfortable with it. Other types of wall decorations are also becoming popular. On the following pages, you'll find lots of ideas. Some are traditional and others quite modern.

WREATH TYPES

Wreaths are available styled many different ways and created from various materials. The wreaths in FIG. 1-1 are representative of the types available on the market today. The top central wreath has a straw base and is covered with Spanish moss. When commercially purchased, the Spanish moss wreath is wrapped with a monofilament thread to keep all in place.

If you would like to construct your own Spanish moss wreath, simply cover a straw wreath with Spanish moss and insert U-shaped craft pins through the moss and into the wreath form to secure. For best results, add several pins around the wreath.

The wreath on the left side of FIG. 1-1 is formed using excelsior in a tightly packed form. In some cases the center core of these wreaths is straw; in others, the excelsior is so tightly packed that no core is needed. Commercially, it is wrapped with monofilament thread to secure in place. Should you wish to make your own, do it in the same way as described above for Spanish moss, replacing the Spanish moss with excelsior.

The bottom wreath in the photo is made of Styrofoam. It works well for many types of wreath making activities. One drawback is that bare wire will pull out of the Styrofoam. Therefore, when inserting U-shaped craft pins or wire in the wreath, dip them into craft glue first.

The wreath on the right-hand side is made of straw. This is one of the most popular varieties and often is the least expensive. Straw wreaths are available round and in other shapes as well. The photo shows a heart-shaped variety.

Fig. 1-1
Various types and styles of wreaths are available on the market.

MOSS VARIETIES

Moss can be used to cover arranging foam, if it is being used in the design. In other cases, moss is used to completely cover the wreath. Various types of moss are available, each serving different purposes. Choose the one that is best for your needs (FIG. 1-2).

Fig. 1-2
Moss is useful to cover foam in a design.

☐ *Spanish moss* (shown at the left side of FIG. 1-2): This moss is available most often in gray. It is also sold in bright green and other colors. The original gray is the most versatile.

☐ *Excelsior* (shown in the center back of FIG.1-2): Excelsior is made of shredded wood shavings. Bleached is the most popular, although other colors are available.

☐ *Natural moss* (Shown in the center front of FIG. 1-2): This material grows naturally on trees and rocks. It is peeled away, fumigated, and sold commercially. Although available in bright green and other colors, the natural version is the most versatile.

☐ *Iridescent shred* (shown on the right of FIG. 1-2): Formed from iridescent plastic sheets, this material is a perfect accent for special-occasion and some high-style arrangements.

To attach any of the above mosses, simply spread them over the top and down around the sides of the item to be covered. A complete, but thin coat is best. Insert a few craft pins through the moss and into the item you are securing the moss to. Never glue the moss to the item; this will make it difficult to insert flower stems into the foam.

WREATH HANGERS

A simple way to form a hanger for your wreath is to use a craft pin. Bend the ends of both sides up approximately one-third of the way up (see FIG. 1-3). After bending both ends, insert the hanger with an upward motion into the top back side of the wreath's center.

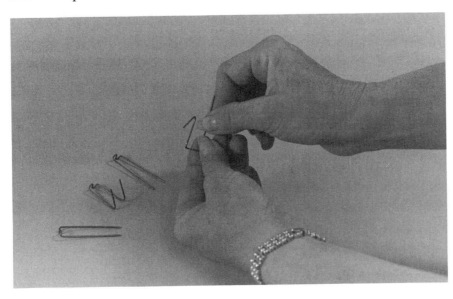

Fig. 1-3
Effective wreath hangers are formed from U-shaped craft pins.

If it is impossible to insert a craft pin in this fashion, you can always wrap 28-gauge wire around the top of the decorative project, forming a loop for hanging.

TOOLS & SUPPLIES

Having the right tools for wreath design is important to the success of your project. Let's discuss the tools you'll need:

☐ *Scissors and wire cutters* (FIG. 1-4): A good set of wire cutters is extremely important. Invest in a top-quality pair, and they will last many years. Wire cutters cut items that are wire or have a wire core.

Fig. 1-4
Good-quality scissors and wire cutters are important design tools.

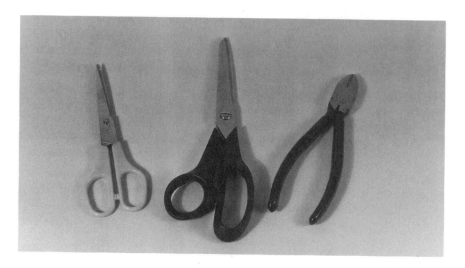

Two different sizes of scissors are shown. Scissors cut non-wire items. Never attempt to cut wire with your good scissors—the blades will get nicked and scratched in a short time, making it impossible to cut ribbon or other items.

☐ *Hot glue gun and glue sticks* (FIG. 1-5): Glue guns are indispensable to floral designers. When proper care is taken, they are fast and easy to use, and offer superior bonding on a number of surfaces.

Glue guns use shaped glue sticks, which are a mixture of plastics, resins, and adhesives. They are inserted into the back of the gun and pass through a heating chamber that melts and activates the glue. The glue gun extrudes quantities of glue, which have been melted to a temperature of 350 degrees. Because of the temperature of the glue, this product should be kept away from children.

Hot melt adhesives form a secure bond within 30 to 90 seconds following application. Most hot melt adhesives will be affected by tem-

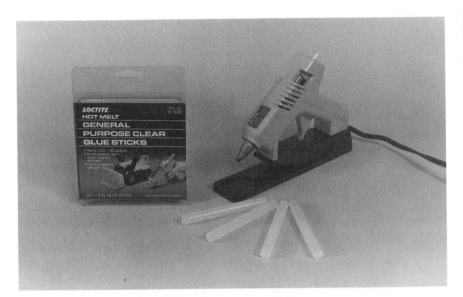

Fig. 1-5
Hot glue guns make wreath
making easier.

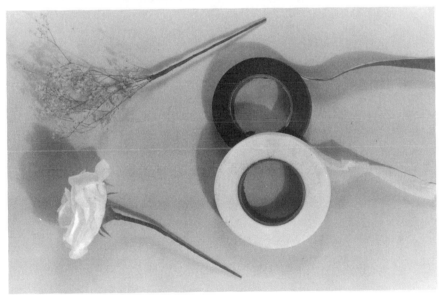

Fig. 1-6
Floral tape helps lengthen
stems and add support to
weak stems.

perature and weather changes and caution should be taken when using them outdoors.

☐ *Floral tape* (FIG. 1-6): Floral tape is a non-sticky tape available in green, white, brown, and a selection of colors. Made of a waxed crepe paper material, floral tape only sticks when it is stretched. It then sticks to itself. The color of the tape should coordinate with the flowers. Choose pastel colors only when green or brown are inappropriate.

Floral tape is useful when lengthening flower stems as well as attaching materials such as clusters of dried flowers to lengths of wire for insertion into the design.

To use: Hold the item or stems to be floral-taped in your left hand. Hold the roll of floral tape in your right hand, with the tape between your thumb and forefinger and the roll of tape resting on your little finger. Wrap the end of the floral tape around the top of the stem and squeeze so the end adheres to the tape and holds the stem.

Begin to twist the stem with your left hand, holding the tape firmly and slightly stretching it with your right hand (FIG. 1-7). The stretching helps to activate the adhesive abilities. Continue to turn the stem, stretching and angling the tape downward as you go. Floral-tape all the way to the end of the stem, breaking and squeezing the tape at the end.

Fig. 1-7
Hold the floral tape in your right hand and the flower stem in your left while wrapping.

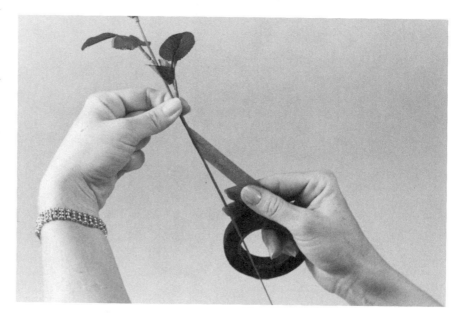

When lengthening or reinforcing stems, use 20-gauge wire the necessary length, and lay the wire next to the item to be taped so that the stems overlap a minimum of 3 inches (7.5 cm). Floral-tape the two together as one.

☐ *Wooden picks* (FIG. 1-8): Wooden picks used in floral design have one blunt end and one pointed end. A wire is attached to the blunt end and is used to wrap around items secured to the pick. The pointed end is then inserted into the design. The photo shows three ways picks are used to assist in wreath making: forming ribbon loops, creating a firm stem for a cluster of dried materials, and lengthening silk flower stems.

Fig. 1-8
Wired wooden picks are a
valuable design aid.

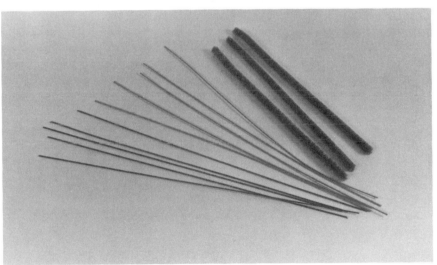

Fig. 1-9
Your workroom should
contain various sizes and
gauges of wire, along with
chenille stems, for securing
bows.

To attach a wood pick: Lay the wired end of the pick against the item, overlapping at least ¹/₂ inch (1.3 cm). Wrap the wire securely around the item and pick a few times, down around the pick only a few times, and then back up and around the item and wood pick again. This will help eliminate twisting and turning on the wood pick.

☐ *Stem wire* (FIG. 1-9): Wire is available in natural gray, as well as green-painted. It is also available in a number of diameters or gauges. The larger the gauge of number identified, the thinner the wire will be.

For example: 30-gauge (ga.) wire is thinner than 16-gauge (ga.) wire.

Green painted wire is usually more costly and most often will end up being floral-taped, so there is no great need to purchase green over natural. Twenty-gauge wire is usually used to lengthen flower stems and help support softer drieds or flowers.

The chenille stems shown on the right of the photo are useful for securing bows and inserting into foams. They are wires twisted with tiny chenille fibers.

ENHANCING FLOWER COLORS

Many colors of flowers are available on the market today, yet sometimes it is difficult to find just the right one to suit your needs. When this happens, the use of a color tool will give you the exact color you desire. Do not use a spray paint; this will make the petals of your flowers very stiff. Instead, use Design Master spray, which is more like a floral dye than a paint. Available in a wide assortment of colors, this spray will leave your flower petals soft to the touch. To use, hold the can away from the flowers and mist the petals with color. Build up the color in steps until the deepest color is achieved (FIG. 1-10).

Fig. 1-10
Design Master Color Tools help enhance the colors of flowers and floral materials.

CARE OF YOUR WREATHS

Taking proper care of your wreaths will ensure a long life to your handiwork. Let's look at some tips and techniques for wreath care:

○ Dust or use a light vacuum tool to keep dust and dirt from building up on your wreath as it is hanging.

○ Always store your wreaths in large plastic bags such as garbage bags.

○ If you have room in a closet, it is good to wire the wreath to a hanger, then cover with dry-cleaning bags.

○ Should your wreath contain bows, stuff the bow loops with polyester stuffing material and they will be fresh as new when you're ready to display them again (FIG. 1-11).

○ If a bow on your wreath has not been stuffed and needs perking up, either hold it over a pot of steaming water or undo the bow and iron the back side.

○ Many types of silk flowers are really made of a polyester material. To make them look as good as new, wash in warm soapy water, then dry with a blow dryer.

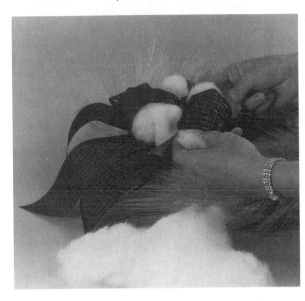

Fig. 1-11
Stuffing your bows with polyester stuffing material helps keep them fresh during storage.

FLOWER TYPES

Three types of flowers exist in design: line, mass, and filler. A selection of line flowers is shown in FIG. 1-12. *Line flowers* are long, thin, tapering materials that are always used at the extremities or outer portions of the design. The purpose of the line flower is to cause your eye to move around the design. Figure 1-12 shows three examples of line flowers: freesia, eucalyptus, and pussy willow.

Mass flowers are round and many-petaled. Usually the main flowers in the design, mass flowers are useful for filling space in the design and can act as the primary feature of the arrangement. Figure 1-13 shows three examples of a mass flower: a rose, a daffodil, and a carnation.

Fig. 1-12 (Above Left) Line flowers draw the viewer's eye through a design.

Fig. 1-13 (Above Right) Mass flowers are usually the main flowers in the design because of their visual weight.

Filler flowers are the third type of flower. The varieties that fit under this heading are endless. Filler flowers are any type of smaller flowers that have many heads on each stem. Their purpose is to add changes of color or texture, or to fill space in the design. Fillers need not be confined to only flowers; materials such as ribbon bows or loops are also considered "fillers." Figure 1-14 shows a stem of silk filler flowers.

PURCHASING YOUR FLOWERS

The material lists for the projects contained in this book list the exact type and style of flower used in the design. You may have trouble finding these materials in their exact configurations. This will happen more often with silk flowers, since many styles are sold in the market. Therefore, when purchasing flowers, be sure to get the number of flowers you need instead of the number of stems listed. For example, if the directions say "two stems of roses with two open flowers and two buds per stem," and your store only has rose stems containing one open and one rosebud, you would need to purchase four stems to get the correct number of flowers.

Figure 1-15 shows one stem of flowers that would be described as "one stem of lilies with two groups each containing three 2 inch (5 cm) open lilies and one bud." Figure 1-14 would be described as "one stem of double silk blossoms with six sprigs of 1-inch (2.5 cm) flowers."

Figure 1-16 shows a stem of eucalyptus that would be described as "one eucalyptus stem with a 12-inch (30.5 cm) leaf portion." This means

Fig. 1-14 (Left)
Filler flowers can be silk
materials or dried flowers.

Fig. 1-15 (Right)
Be sure to purchase the
right number of flowers as
called for in the materials
list.

that the measurement you would need should be taken of the leaf portion only. The stem is not included in this measurement. If the instructions call for "a 14- inch (35 cm) eucalyptus stem," you would measure the entire stem from the tip all the way down to the end of the stem.

Figure 1-17 shows a number of varieties of materials that are very useful in designing wreaths. Remember that you can use your imagination and change the materials we suggest in the book to create a look uniquely your own.

Fig. 1-16 (Below Left)
When a leaf portion is
given, measure the length
from the tip of the stem to
the bottom leaf.

Fig. 1-17 (Below Right)
Many other materials can
add interest and texture
contrast in your design.

CHAPTER 2

Ribbons
& Bows

*T*his chapter deals with the many wonderful, creative things you can do with ribbon to enhance your wreath designs. Ribbons are available in a multitude of widths, colors, and textures. You can find something to enhance any project you create.

RIBBON LOOPS

To form a ribbon loop: Cut a piece of ribbon the length indicated in the directions, bring the ends together, and lay a wood pick next to the ends of the ribbon. Then wrap the wire snugly around the ribbon ends and the wood pick. For a single streamer of ribbon, simply attach a wood pick to the end of a piece of ribbon in the same manner as described above. See FIG. 2-1 to see how these are done.

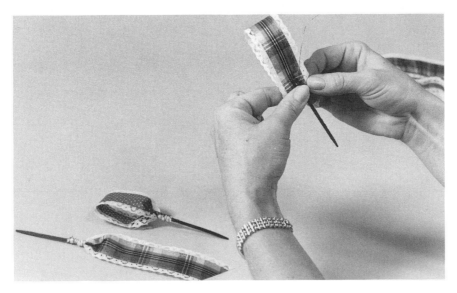

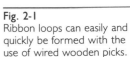

Fig. 2-1
Ribbon loops can easily and quickly be formed with the use of wired wooden picks.

Fig. 2-2
The basic craft bow is one of the most frequently made bows for wreath decoration.

BASIC BOW

Fig. 2-3 (Below Left)
The first step in forming a basic bow is to make a loop.

Fig. 2-4 (Below Right)
If the ribbon has a right and wrong side, completely twist the ribbon until the right side is showing.

To form the type of bow pictured in FIG. 2-2, begin by cutting a length of ribbon as indicated in the directions. Form a loop of ribbon the size necessary and hold it between the thumb and forefinger of your left hand (FIG. 2-3). If you are using a ribbon that has a right and wrong side, twist the bottom portion of the ribbon so that you see the right side (FIG. 2-4).

Form a second loop with the lower portion of ribbon, bringing it to the back and pinching between your thumb and forefinger (FIG. 2-5).

Again twist the ribbon to see the right side and form a third loop. Continue in this fashion during the construction of one more loop.

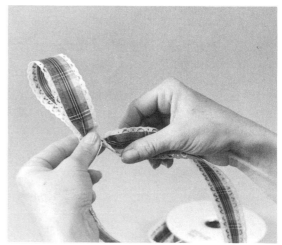

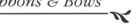

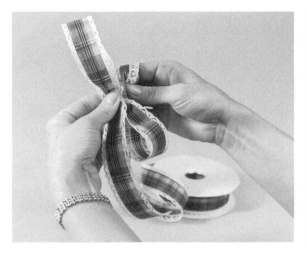

After you have one-half the loops you are making, add the loop in the center. To do this, simply form a small loop of ribbon around your thumb as shown in FIG. 2-6 and pinch the back portion of ribbon again between your thumb and forefinger.

Continue adding at least four loops, or more if desired, in the same manner as described above. When finished, insert a cloth-covered wire or chenille stem through the center loop. Bring the ends to the back and twist securely.

Fig. 2-5 (Above Left) Form a second loop at the bottom of the bow.

Fig. 2-6 (Above Right) The center loop is added halfway through and is made by wrapping the ribbon around your thumb.

LAYERED BOW

A natural progression after the basic bow is a lovely bow style we call the layered bow (FIG. 2-7). Throughout this book, you will find several times where two bows are used together in a design. This adds a great deal of contrast, texture, and color to the project.

After mastering the basic bow, the layered bow is simple! Make two basic bows as shown in FIG. 2-8. The one on the left will be the top bow. Its loops are slightly shorter than the back bow, and it has a center loop that was made from the basic bow instructions. The bow on the right is the one that will be behind. Its loops are slightly larger and it has no center loop. To duplicate this, follow all the instructions for the basic bow leaving out the step for making the center loop.

Both bows are secured with either cloth-covered wire or a chenille stem. Insert the stems of the top bow through the loops of the bottom bow as shown in FIG. 2-9. Bring all the wires together behind, twisting them all together and securing the bows into one unit (FIG. 2-10). More than two layers can be used by simply wiring as many bows as you wish, one on top of the other. Only the top bow should have a center loop; leave that step off of every other bow.

Fig. 2-7 (Above Left)
The layered bow is an attractive bow that highlights ribbons of various colors and textures.

Fig. 2-8 (Above Right)
The layered bow is made with two basic bows, one having no center loop.

TAILORED BOW

As you'll note in the photo, this bow has a longer, more narrow appearance when compared to the basic bow (FIG. 2-11).

To form this bow, you will be making a series of cylinders of ribbon. Each layer is a different length so that when stacked, they give a stair-step effect. To form the cylinders, cut a length of ribbon, bringing the ends together and overlapping approximately 2 inches (5 cm) (FIG. 2-12).

Form a series of smaller cylinders and stack on top of each other as shown in FIG. 2-13. Lift this grouping and pinch together from both sides in the center of the bow (FIG. 2-14). Lay a length of ribbon the length desired on the back of the bow and insert a chenille stem through the

Fig. 2-9 (Left)
Insert the chenille stems of the top bow through the loops of the bottom bow.

Fig. 2-10 (Right)
Twist all the chenille stem ends together to secure.

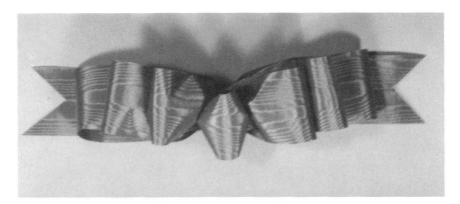

Fig. 2-11
A tailored bow suggests elegance.

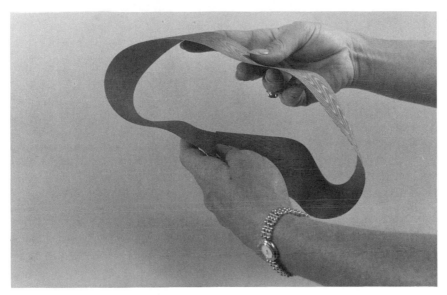

Fig. 2-12
The first step in forming a tailored bow is to form a ribbon cylinder.

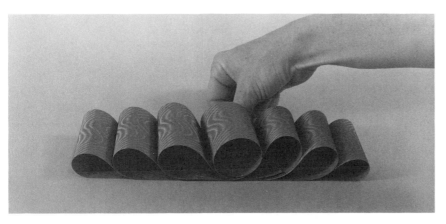

Fig. 2-13
Several cylinders of different sizes should be stacked.

Fig. 2-14
Pinch the center back of the
stacked ribbon loops.

Fig. 2-15
Insert a chenille stem
through the center of the
bow.

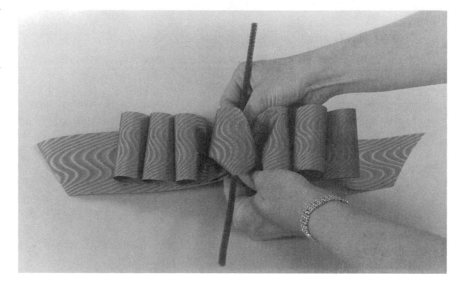

center (FIG. 2-15). Now bring both ends to the back of the bow, catching all loops and streamers, and twist the ends together tightly.

RIBBON BRAIDING

Braided ribbon adds a lovely accent to many finished designs. The procedure is the same as braiding hair. Begin by securing the ends of the three pieces of ribbon. This can be done with cloth-covered wire as shown in FIG. 2-16 or simply staple the three together.

To braid: Bring the left ribbon over the center ribbon. The left ribbon is now the center ribbon. Bring the right ribbon over the center ribbon. The right ribbon is now the center ribbon (FIG. 2-17). Repeat this process for the length of the ribbon requested, then secure the other ends of the ribbons with wire or staples.

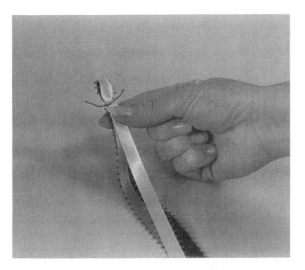

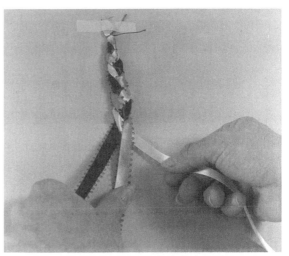

RIBBON FANS

Ribbon fans are very easy to create and can be made many different sizes with different widths of ribbon (FIG. 2-18). To form the fans, cut the ribbon the length specified in the instructions. Accordion-pleat each piece, using ½-inch (1.3 cm) pleats. After pleating, wrap a length of cloth-covered wire around one end to secure it. Allow the other end to fan out. The longer you cut the ribbon, the fuller the fan will be.

Fig. 2-16 (Above Left) Secure the ends of three ribbons together when beginning to braid.

Fig. 2-17 (Above Right) Outside ribbons over center ribbon is the technique for braiding.

Fig. 2-18 Ribbon fans are easily made by accordion-pleating a wide ribbon and securing the end with a piece of cloth-covered wire.

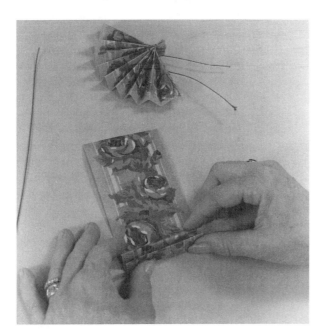

POTPOURRI SACKS

Fig. 2-19 (Below Left)
To form a potpourri sack, place a walnut-sized bunch of potpourri into the center of a square of tulle.

Fig. 2-20 (Below Right)
Pinch the ends of the tulle square together to form a sack.

Potpourri sacks are wonderful, fragrant accents to any wreath design. All you need is a square of tulle or illusion usually 6 inches (15 cm) wide. Choose the type of potpourri that will best enhance the type of wreath you are making; rose is wonderful for romantic wreath styles, cinnamon works better in projects featuring apples.

Place a walnut-sized bunch of potpourri in the center of the illusion square (FIG. 2-19). Bring the ends of the tulle up into a cluster held between your fingers (FIG. 2-20). Wrap the sack with a 12-inch (30.5 cm) length of ribbon to secure together.

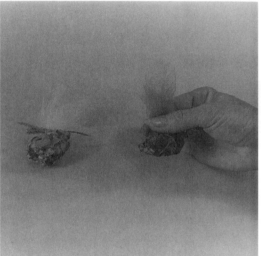

RIBBON OR FABRIC SHIRRING

Shirring a wreath with ribbon or fabric is a lovely change from the traditional ways we accent our wreaths, and it is so easy to do! Figure 2-21 shows how this beautiful technique looks after completion.

If you are using a lace-type ribbon or fabric to shir, it is best to completely wrap the wreath first with a solid color moiré or satin ribbon. This gives a background color to the lace and hides the unsightly bare wreath.

Wrap an 8-inch (20 cm) width of ribbon or fabric width-wise around the wreath, pinning the ends behind the wreath (FIG. 2-22). Turn the wreath right-side-over again, and grab both sides of the ribbon as shown in FIG. 2-23. Pull these two sections down, forming a gather in the ribbon (FIG. 2-24). Pin these sections to the back of the wreath. Continue grabbing, moving down, and pinning until the entire wreath is covered.

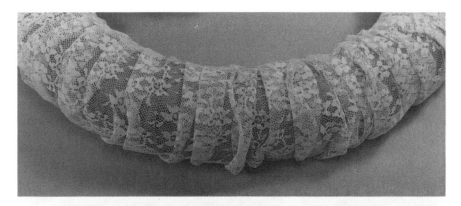

Fig. 2-21
Shirring ribbon or fabric creates a lush, full look.

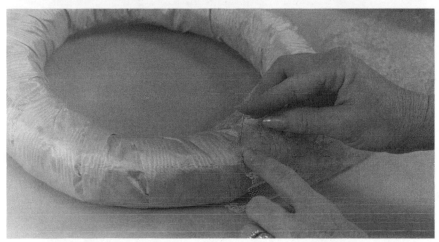

Fig. 2-22
To begin shirring, pin the ends to the back of the wreath.

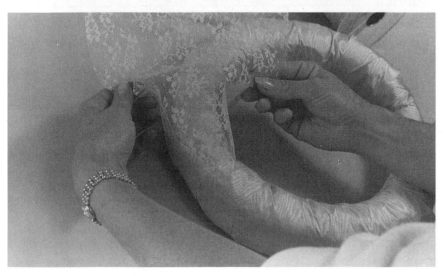

Fig. 2-23
On the top side, hold the sides of the lace with both hands and pull it downward to gather.

Fig. 2-24
Pinch the ribbon into the
wreath and secure behind
with pins.

TWISTED RIBBON TECHNIQUE

This lovely technique adds another look to an ordinary wreath (FIG. 2-25). You can simply do the twisted ribbon portion of the instructions, allowing some of the bare wreath to show through. Or you can completely cover the wreath first with a coordinating solid or pattern ribbon before doing the twisted ribbon technique.

Fig. 2-25
The twisted ribbon tech-
nique creates a unique look
to a plain wreath.

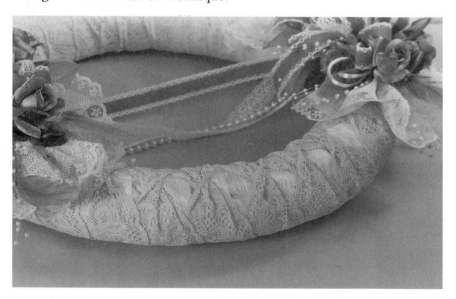

To begin: Secure one end of the ribbon to the back of the wreath with a craft pin. Wrap the ribbon around to the front of the wreath. Hold the ribbon snugly in the center on the top of the wreath with your finger. Twist the ribbon a complete turn so that the right side is still facing up (FIG. 2-26).

Wrap the ribbon around the back of the wreath and again to the front. Repeat the steps in the paragraph above until the entire wreath is covered (FIG. 2-27).

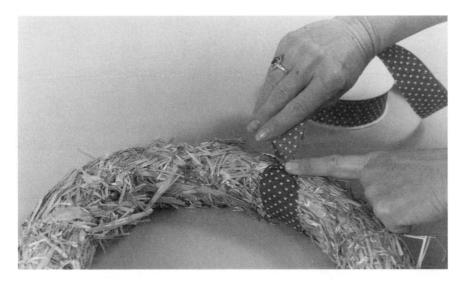

Fig. 2-26
To begin, wrap the ribbon to the center top of the wreath and hold down with your finger while twisting the ribbon.

Fig. 2-27
Continue to wrap the wreath, and twist the ribbon until the wreath is completely covered.

CHAPTER 3

Kitchen Wreaths

*T*he kitchen, as the central location for all family activity, is a delightful place to decorate. Kitchen wreath designs can feature edible items such as cookies for a unique touch, or can be decorated with items normally used in the kitchen such as pot holders or wooden spoons.

Since so much time is spent in the kitchen, it is the perfect room to think of when designing a gift for someone special. They will see your gift daily and certainly appreciate the time and effort you put into creating something just right for them.

PRESERVING APPLES

You can purchase ready-to-use preserved apples from a craft shop, or you can preserve your own.

If you wish to do your own, you will need to purchase a bottle of glycerin. Check your local drugstore. Slice fresh apples approximately 1/4 inch thick (.6 cm) and soak in the glycerin for approximately 20 minutes.

After removing the apples from the glycerin solution, air-dry them on screens for a few days. As soon as they are dry, you must spray them with an acrylic craft spray to seal. Spraying will prevent them from turning moldy.

Prepare as many apples as you would like—they keep for quite a while when done properly. After being displayed for some time, the apples may take on a golden brown tone instead of the white, bleached look following glycerine treatment. This is a beautiful change and can actually enhance your apple project.

The following projects were created using preserved apples. If you have any apple slices left over, they are a lovely accent when added to a wicker basket filled with apple potpourri or pieces of dried baby's breath.

APPLES GALORE WREATH

The eye movement created with the use of the diagonal ribbon is very appealing and exciting for the viewer (FIG. 3-1).

You will need:

- ☐ One 17-inch (43 cm) excelsior wreath
- ☐ 7¹/₂ yards (6.8 m) 2-inch-wide (5 cm) red country apple print ribbon
- ☐ Two 12-inch (30.5 cm) wooden spoons
- ☐ 2-ounce bag gray-painted gypsophila
- ☐ Thirteen preserved apple slices, each approx. 2¹/₂ inches (6.5 cm) wide
- ☐ Thirteen wired wooden picks
- ☐ Two eggshell chenille stems
- ☐ U-shaped craft pins
- ☐ Hot glue gun and sticks
- ☐ White craft glue

1. First, wrap the wreath in a spiral fashion with 2¹/₂ yards (2.3 m) of the 2-inch-wide (5 cm) country apple print ribbon. Secure the ends of the ribbon to the wreath with the use of a craft pin and glue.

2. Following the instructions in chapter 2, form a basic bow with 4 yards (3.6 m) of ribbon. The bow should have eight 5-inch-long (12.5 cm) loops, and 18-inch (45.5 cm) streamers. Secure with a chenille stem.

3. Attach the bow to the upper-right corner of the wreath by wrapping the chenille stem ends around the wreath and twisting them together in the back of the wreath. Bring the bow streamers down to the lower left corner of the wreath, using craft pins and glue. Secure these streamers in place.

4. With the remaining ribbon, form a four-loop bow, each loop measuring 4 inches (10 cm) and having no streamers. Secure this bow with the other chenille stem and use to wrap around the wreath over the streamer ends on the lower left of the wreath.

5. Glue two wooden spoons following the ribbon streamers down the center of the wreath. The handles of the spoons should be glued into the center loop of the bow. One spoon should be placed 3 inches (7.5 cm) lower than the other spoon.

6. Break off 2-inch (5 cm) to 4-inch (10 cm) pieces of painted gypsophila and dip each end into tacky glue. Insert these pieces throughout the bow loops. Continue adding pieces of gypsophila until the desired fullness is achieved.

7. Remove the wire on the end of the wooden pick and glue the pick to the back of an apple slice, overlapping 1 inch (2.5 cm) onto the apple. Repeat this step for all the apple slices. When they are dry, glue seven of these prepared apples into the top bow throughout the bow loops by applying glue to the wood pick before inserting into place. Repeat this procedure and glue six apple slices into the bottom bow loops. Attach a wreath hanger of your choice following the instructions in chapter 1.

SLICED APPLE RING

Simple to create and lovely to look at, this wreath is a great gift item (FIG. 3-2).

You will need:

☐ One 8-inch-diameter (20 cm) cardboard wreath ring

☐ Nine preserved apple slices, each approx. 2¹/₂ inches (6.5 cm) wide

☐ 1¹/₂ yards (1.3 m) of ⁷/₈-inch-wide (2 cm) red apple print ribbon

☐ Two 3-inch (7.5 cm) pieces eggshell chenille stem

☐ Hot glue gun and sticks

1. Glue apples around the cardboard wreath ring, overlapping the apple edges by ¹/₂ inch (1.3 cm) to fit them around the wreath.

Fig. 3-2
Over time, preserved apples turn a deep golden color.

2. Following the instructions in chapter 2, make a ten-loop bow, with each loop being approximately 2 inches (5 cm). The bow should have 4-inch (10 cm) streamers. Glue the bow to the top of the wreath.

3. Form a loop from a 3-inch (7.5 cm) length of chenille stem and glue to the back of the cardboard ring as a hanger.

APPLE & CINNAMON WREATH

When the kitchen becomes warm from the preparation of a meal, the heat and humidity may cause this wreath to emit a soft cinnamon fragrance (FIG. 3-3).

You will need:

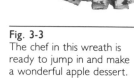

- ☐ One 12-inch (30.5 cm) flat or half-round Styrofoam wreath
- ☐ 1 pound cinnamon sticks
- ☐ 2 yards (1.8 m) of 3-inch-wide (7.5 cm) country-house-print ribbon
- ☐ 4 yards (3.6 m) of 1¹/₂-inch-wide (4 cm) French blue gauze-like ribbon
- ☐ 2¹/₂ yards (2.3 m) untwisted French blue whitewashed paper ribbon
- ☐ 1¹/₂ yards (1.3 m) rust untwisted paper ribbon
- ☐ 1¹/₂ yards (1.3 m) natural untwisted paper ribbon
- ☐ Four 3-inch (7.5 cm) preserved apple slices
- ☐ One 6-inch (15 cm) chef figure
- ☐ Hot glue gun and sticks
- ☐ 1-inch (2.5 cm) straight pins
- ☐ stapler and staples
- ☐ two chenille stems

Fig. 3-3
The chef in this wreath is ready to jump in and make a wonderful apple dessert.

1. Begin by completely wrapping the wreath with the 1¹/₂-inch-wide (4 cm) French blue gauze-like ribbon, pinning the ends to secure. Following the box pleat instructions with FIG. 6-10 on page 89, staple-pleat the ribbon, using the 3-inch- wide (7.5 cm) ribbon. Each pleat should be 2 inches (5 cm) wide. Using the straight pins, attach this pleat around the outside back of the wreath.

2. Break the cinnamon sticks into 4-inch (10 cm) pieces. Glue these pieces side-by-side all around the top edge of the wreath. Braid 1¹/₂ yards (1.3 m) each of the untwisted paper ribbons together, securing the ends with 1¹/₂-inch (4 cm) pieces of chenille stem. Follow the instructions in chapter 2 to braid. Glue this braid around the center of the cinnamon

sticks on the top of the wreath. The braid ends should meet at approximately 9 o'clock on the wreath.

3. Untwist the remaining one yard of French blue whitewashed paper ribbon. The easiest way to do this is to soak the ribbon in warm water for a few minutes before untwisting. You can construct the bow when the ribbon is wet, or lay it out to dry first.

4. The bow should have four 3-inch (7.5 cm) loops with no center loop, and two 6-inch (15 cm) streamers. Secure the bow with a 3-inch (7.5 cm) length of chenille stem and glue into place over the ends of the braid on the left side of the wreath.

5. Glue the chef into the center of the bow and the four apple slices equally spaced around the remainder of the wreath.

PRESERVING COOKIES & ROLLS

Cookies and rolls can be a very effective addition to wreaths designed for the kitchen. Although this type of wreath cannot be stored and reused from year to year, the look and, at times, aroma of these products make them very worthwhile to prepare.

A high-gloss spray or brush-on sealer will effectively seal these items from dust and dirt while prolonging their display life. Cookies can be either purchased or baked in your own kitchen. To preserve, apply several coats of sealer to the front and back of the cookies, taking care to fill in all nooks and indentations. When dry, they can be arranged as discussed.

The rolls can also be purchased or prepared in your own kitchen. They will preserve best if they are slow-dried in an oven before they are sealed. To do this, simply place purchased rolls on a cookie sheet in a 225 degree oven for approximately 1½ to 2 hours or until they are dried throughout. After they cool, spray with a high-gloss sealer or paint on a liquid sealer. Both are available in most craft shops.

If you are preparing the dough for the rolls, use a slow temperature (approx. 200 degrees) and bake until rolls are firm and dried throughout. Seal as described above.

The breadsticks used in the following design were already a firmer bread and did not need to be dried in the oven. Simply seal with a spray or brush on as discussed.

FIESTA BREAD WREATH

Choose various types and sizes of rolls to add the most interesting and unique texture contrasts (FIG. 3-4).

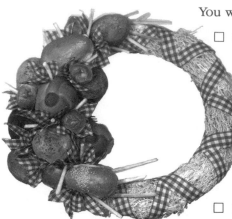

You will need:

- [ ] One 16-inch (40.5 cm) excelsior wreath
- [ ] Five 1¹⁄₂-inch (4 cm) purchased rolls
- [ ] Ten 4-inch (10 cm) to 5-inch (12.5 cm) large purchased rolls in assorted varieties
- [ ] Nine 9-inch (22.5 cm) × ³⁄₈-inch-wide (1.2 cm) breadsticks
- [ ] 6 yards (5.4 m) 1¹⁄₂-inch-wide (4 cm) red gingham ribbon
- [ ] 3¹⁄₂ yards (3.2 m) 3-inch-wide (7.5 cm) red gingham ribbon
- [ ] High-gloss sealer
- [ ] Hot glue gun and sticks
- [ ] Fourteen 3-inch (7.5 cm) pieces white chenille stem
- [ ] U-shaped craft pins

1. Using 3 yards (2.7 m) of 1¹⁄₂-inch-wide (4 cm) ribbon, spiral-wrap the wreath and secure the ribbon ends with a craft pin and glue. Using the second 3 yards (2.7 m), similarly wrap the wreath in the opposite direction so that an X-pattern appears with the ribbon.

2. Glue the large rolls in a crescent pattern along the left side of the wreath. Glue the smaller rolls randomly among the larger rolls.

3. Cut fourteen 8-inch (20 cm) lengths of the 3-inch-wide (7.5 cm) ribbon. Fold the end of the ribbon in half width wise and cut at an angle from the fold up to the point. When open, the end of the ribbon will have a V-shaped cut. Repeat for the other end of the ribbon. Pinch the middle of the ribbon together and wrap this section with one of the chenille stems. Continue making all fourteen ribbon tufts.

4. Add glue to the twisted chenille stem end and insert ribbon tufts throughout the rolls on the wreath.

5. Next, fill between the rolls and ribbon pieces with pieces of the bread sticks, also glueing in place.

COOKIES & . . . MORE COOKIES WREATH

Cookies, cookies, and more cookies of various colors and textures make this a delightfully fun project to create for the kitchen (FIG. 3-5).
    You will need:

- [ ] One 16-inch-square (40.5 cm), ¹⁄₄-inch-thick (.6 cm) cardboard or foam-centered board
- [ ] 6 yards (5.4 m) of ⁷⁄₈-inch-wide (2 cm) heart stencil patterned ribbon

- ☐ Twenty-eight 3-inch-wide (7.5 cm) cookies of various types
- ☐ Fourteen 2-inch-wide (5 cm) square and round chocolate-iced cookies
- ☐ Six 3-inch (7.5 cm) eggshell chenille stems
- ☐ White craft glue
- ☐ One U-shaped craft pin
- ☐ X-acto knife, pencil, ruler

1. Using the pattern in FIG. 3-6, cut a circle out of the cardboard. Glue a row of fourteen cookies end-to-end around the wreath. Glue a second row of fourteen cookies, overlapping the first row, by staggering a cookie over a space between two cookies in the first row.

2. Glue the smaller cookies in a third row around the wreath. Each cookie should be placed on top of the section where two cookies of the second row meet.

Fig. 3-5
Cookies, cookies, and more cookies . . . a fun wreath to make!

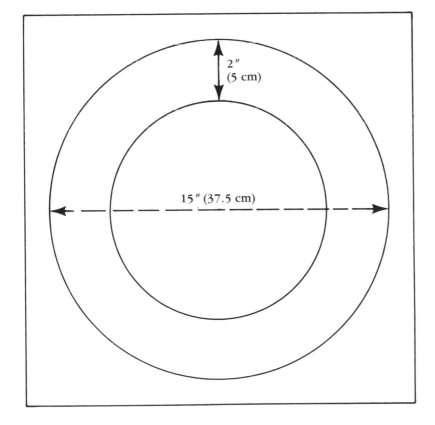

2″
(5 cm)

15″ (37.5 cm)

Fig. 3-6
Cut this frame from foam board or cardboard.

3. Following instructions in chapter 2, form a six-loop bow with 1 yard (.9 m) of ribbon, each loop measuring 2 inches (5 cm). Secure with a chenille stem piece. Continue making a total of six bows in the same manner.

4. Glue the bows equally spaced around the wreath. When dry, attach a wreath hanger as described in chapter 1.

VEGETABLE GARDEN WREATH

The realistic look of the new silk vegetables is amazing. This design looks fresh enough to eat (FIG. 3-7)!

Fig. 3-7
This wonderful whitewashed design looks fresh and new.

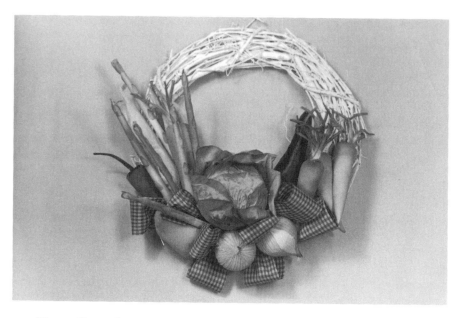

You will need:

☐ One 16-inch (40.5 cm) white-painted grapevine wreath
☐ Two 8-inch (20 cm) ears of silk corn
☐ Four 6-inch (15 cm) silk carrots
☐ One 7-inch (17.5 cm) silk eggplant
☐ Two 4-inch (10 cm) silk onions
☐ One 5-inch-wide (12.5 cm) head of silk lettuce
☐ Six 9-inch (22.5 cm) silk asparagus stems
☐ One 5-inch (12.5 cm) silk red pepper
☐ One 4½-inch (11.3 cm) silk potato
☐ 2 yards (1.8 m) of 3-inch-wide (7.5 cm) blue gingham ribbon

☐ Eight 3-inch (7.5 cm) chenille stems

☐ Hot glue gun and glue

1. With the hot glue gun and sticks, attach a head of lettuce to the center bottom of the wreath. Glue one of the onions directly below the lettuce and one placed slightly to the right. Attach the eggplant by glueing along the inside curve on the right of the wreath.

2. The three carrots should be glued in a bunch along the right side of the wreath. Place the potato below and to the left of the lettuce head. The red pepper, last carrot, corn, and asparagus spears should be glued along the left side of the wreath in a random fashion, giving the appearance of a cluster of vegetables.

3. Cut the ribbon into eight pieces, each 8 inches (20 cm) long. Form each into a loop by bringing the ribbon ends together, gathering both ends together, and wrapping with one 3-inch (7.5 cm) length of chenille stem. Repeat to form all eight loops.

4. Glue these loops throughout the vegetables, placing them so that they fill space between each.

WELCOME TO MY KITCHEN WREATH

The delightful kitchen items used to decorate this wreath make it a perfect gift for a shower or new home. Since the kitchen pieces can then be removed and used, this treatment also makes an effective and unique gift wrap (FIG. 3-8).

You will need:

☐ One set measuring spoons

☐ One set measuring cups

☐ One large oven mitt

☐ One narrow spatula

☐ One wide spatula

☐ One dish towel with home design

☐ One 12-inch (30.5 cm) straw wreath

☐ 6-ounce package bleached preserved gypsophila

☐ Approximately eight 6-inch (15 cm) to 8-inch (20 cm) stems preserved huckleberry

☐ 1-ounce package purple statice sinuata

☐ 1-ounce package white statice sinuata

☐ Ten red dried Holland roses, each head measuring 1¹/₂ inches (4 cm)

Continued

Fig. 3-8
The kitchen gadgets attached to the wreath can then be removed and used by the hostess.

☐ Four lengths blue glittered ting ting approximately 40 inches (1 m) long

☐ 5 yards (4.5 m) ¹/₂-inch-wide (1.3 cm) mauve picot ribbon

☐ 5 yards (4.5 m) ¹/₂-inch-wide (1.3 cm) French blue picot ribbon

☐ 3-inch (7.5 cm) corsage pins

☐ U-shaped craft pins

☐ 28-gauge white cloth-covered wire

☐ Hot glue and gun

☐ Green floral tape

1. Break off 3-inch (7.5 cm) to 4-inch (10 cm) pieces of gypsophila to form clusters. Using craft pins, pin over the cluster stems and into the wreath. Continue forming clusters and pinning to the wreath, working the clusters side-by-side with new rows covering the stems of the previous rows. Continue until the wreath is completely covered.

2. Starting at approximately a 1 o'clock position on the wreath, glue eight huckleberry stems, forming an oval shape on the wreath approximately 10 inches (25.5 cm) tall. Break the stems of the roses, purple statice, and white statice to approximately a 1-inch (2.5 cm) length.

Glue these pieces randomly throughout the huckleberry oval, filling the space between the gypsophila.

3. Using the ting ting, form loops approximately 6 inches (15 cm) in length. Wrap the ends of the loops with wire and further secure with floral tape. Glue loops throughout the floral oval. The ends of the ting ting add an extra-special flair when they are glued near the ting ting loops following the curve of the wreath.

4. Form a bow using 3 yards (2.7 m) of the blue ribbon and 3 yards (2.7 m) of the mauve ribbon together in one bow. The bow should have thirteen 3-inch (7.5 cm) loops and have 10-inch (25.5 cm) streamers. Form a second bow using 2 yards (1.8 m) of each color ribbon with ten 2 1/2-inch (6.5 cm) loops and with 5-inch (12.5 cm) streamers. Pin and glue the 3-yard (2.7 m) bow under the dried materials. Swag the streamers of the bow over to the left side of the wreath and pin and glue them in place at approximately a 9 o'clock position. Place the 2-yard (1.8 m) bow at the top of the floral oval.

5. Wrap a length of cloth-covered wire around the center of the towel and then around the center of the left side of the wreath to secure. Using corsage pins inserted inside the oven mitt and into the wreath, position the mitt in place over the end of the towel.

6. Use craft pins to secure the spoons, spatulas, and measuring cups in place around the mitt and towel. These pieces can then be removed from the wreath and used by the hostess of the house.

WHEAT & GARLIC WREATH

Garlic is said to ward off evil spirits and is used in this design to create a delightful kitchen wreath (FIG. 3-9).

You will need:

☐ One 10-inch (25.5 cm) straw wreath

☐ Eighteen pieces wheat

☐ 1-ounce package small orange dried flowers

☐ Ten large whole garlic heads

☐ 4 yards (3.6 m) of 1 1/2-inch-wide (4 cm) hunter-green heart ribbon to wrap wreath

☐ 2 yards (1.8 m) 1 1/2-inch-wide (4 cm) country print ribbon for bow

☐ U-shaped craft pins

☐ Hot glue gun and sticks

1. Begin by securing the end of the 1 1/2-inch-wide (4 cm) hunter-green ribbon to the back of the wreath with a craft pin. Wrap the ribbon

Fig. 3-9
Garlic is said to ward off the evil spirits.

around to the front of the wreath. Hold the ribbon snugly in the center on the top of the wreath with your thumb.

2. Twist the ribbon a complete turn so the right side is still facing up. Wrap the ribbon around the back of the wreath and to the front of the wreath again.

3. Repeat the twisting method on the front of the wreath as previously described. Continue until the entire wreath is covered. Secure the other end of the ribbon to the back of the wreath with a craft pin.

4. Following the instructions in chapter 2, make a basic bow, using the 2 yards (1.8 m) of country print ribbon and forming ten 3½-inch (8.8 cm) loops with two 10-inch (25.5 cm) streamers. Attach the bow to the top of the wreath with craft pins and glue. Pin the streamers to the bottom of the wreath at approximately 5 o'clock and 7 o'clock on the wreath.

5. To attach the garlic, glue one head in the center of the bow and one on the pinned location of each streamer. Continue by glueing garlic heads throughout the bow loops and one down each ribbon streamer.

6. The wheat heads should be cut with approximately 1-inch (2.5 cm) to 2-inch (5 cm) stems remaining. Glue three wheat heads under the gar-

lic head on each streamer attached to the wreath. Continue glueing wheat heads throughout the bow loops at the top of the wreath.

7. Break the dried flower pieces into 3-inch (7.5 cm) to 6-inch (15 cm) lengths. Glue these throughout the bow loops and under the garlic heads on the bow streamers. Following instructions in chapter 1, add a hanger to the back of the wreath.

BARNYARD EGGS-GO-ROUND WREATH

In this fun-to-create wreath, ordinary chicken wire is used to enclose plastic eggs and form a circular wreath (FIG. 3-10).

You will need:

☐ 36-inch (.9 m) × 6-inch (15 cm) piece chicken wire

☐ Eleven 2-inch (5 cm) white plastic eggs

☐ One 5-inch (12.5 cm) hen

☐ One 5-inch (12.5 cm) rooster

☐ 3 yards (2.7 m) of 1½-inch-wide (4 cm) blue mini dot ribbon with a lace edge

☐ 1½ yards (1.3 m) of 3-inch-wide (7.5 cm) country house ribbon

☐ Two chenille stems

☐ Hot glue gun and sticks

1. Roll the chicken wire into a cylinder 36 inches (.9 m) long. Insert the eggs every two inches and squeeze the chicken wire on either side of the egg to secure in place. Twist the wires around each other to secure all in place.

2. Form the cylinder into a circular wreath and again, twist the wire ends together to secure.

3. Wrap 24 inches (60.5 cm) of 1½-inch-wide (4 cm) ribbon around the wreath and glue ends together. This is the center ribbon in the photograph. Next, glue one 10-inch (25.5 cm) strip of ribbon from the bottom of the center ribbon and up to each side of the wreath, glued at an angle and forming a V.

4. Form a four-loop bow with the 3-inch-wide (7.5 cm) ribbon having each loop 5½ inches (13.8 cm) long with 9-inch (22.5 cm) streamers. Attach this bow with the chenille stem to the base of the wreath where all ribbons come together.

5. Form a six-loop bow with 4-inch (10 cm) loops and 8½-inch (21.3 cm) streamers. Wire this bow to the center of the first bow.

6. Glue the hen and rooster into the center of the wreath among the bow loops.

Fig. 3-10
A new twist in the use of chicken wire is in use here with plastic eggs.

HOT PEPPER WREATH

Normally we use hot peppers in our cooking pots, but in this design we are decorating the kitchen with them (FIG. 3-11).

You will need:

☐ One 8¹/₂-inch (21.3 cm) twig heart wreath

☐ 1-ounce bag white statice sinuata

☐ Six dried chili peppers, 5 inches (12.5 cm) to 7 inches (15.5 cm) long

☐ 3¹/₂ yards (3.2 m) of ¹/₂-inch-wide (1.3 cm) rust mini dot ribbon

☐ Hot glue gun and sticks

1. Loosely wrap the wreath with the ribbon in a spiral fashion, securing the ends with glue.

2. With 1¹/₂ yards (1.3 m) of ribbon, form a bow having twelve 3-inch (7.5 cm) loops. Glue the bow to the top of the heart wreath. Glue one pepper to each side of the bow and fill between chili and bow loops with 1 inch (2.5 cm) stems of statice.

3. Glue one pepper to the point at the base of the wreath. Glue 1-inch (2.5 cm) stems of statice around the pepper.

4. Cut a 5-inch (12.5 cm) ribbon length, a 7¹/₂-inch (18.8 cm) ribbon length, and a 15-inch (38 cm) ribbon length. Glue all three behind the point on the heart wreath. Glue one pepper to each ribbon streamer. Following instructions in chapter 1, attach a wreath hanger to the back of the wreath.

Fig. 3-11
Although we love chili peppers in our cooking, we can also enjoy them used in a decorative manner.

SCRAMBLED EGGS KITCHEN WREATH

This cute kitchen design uses wooden spoons as the main focus for the silk flowers and plastic eggs (FIG. 3-12).

You will need:

☐ One 16-inch (40.5 cm) grapevine wreath

☐ 5¹/₂ yards (5 m) of ⁷/₈-inch-wide (2 cm) red gingham ribbon

☐ 2 yards (1.8 m) of ⁵/₈-inch-wide (1.5 cm) blue heart ribbon

☐ Two 14-inch-long (35 cm) red geranium droopers

☐ Five yellow azalea stems with two 2-inch (5 cm) flowers per stem

☐ One stem deep blue double blossoms with six sprigs of four 1-inch (2.5 cm) flowers each

☐ Six 2-inch (5 cm) white eggs on stems

☐ Two 12-inch (30.5 cm) wooden spoons

☐ Two 3-inch (7.5 cm) chenille stems

☐ 3-inch (7.5 cm) pieces of 28-gauge cloth-covered wire

☐ Hot glue gun and sticks

1. Spiral-wrap the wreath with the red gingham ribbon. Secure the ends with glue.

2. Cut the stem of one geranium drooper to 1 inch (2.5 cm) and attach by glueing the cut end to the bottom of the wreath just left of the center. Lay the remainder of the geranium stem along the left side of the wreath and secure in a few places with lengths of cloth-covered wire.

3. Repeat with a second geranium drooper, glueing the stem to the right of the first stem and attaching the drooper along the bottom and up the right side of the wreath.

4. Cut azalea stems to 1 inch (2.5 cm) and glue stems into the wreath between geraniums so the flowers are distributed throughout the wreath. Cut the sprigs of the double blossom stem apart singly and glue throughout the other flowers.

5. Following the instructions in chapter 2, form an eight-loop bow with 3-inch (7.5 cm) loops and 12-inch (30.5 cm) streamers, and secure with a chenille stem. Repeat forming a second bow with the blue ribbon. Glue the red bow to the wreath at the location where both stem ends join. Attach the blue bow on top of the red one. Bring one red and one blue streamer through the flowers on the left side of the wreath, glueing in a few locations to the leaves of the flowers. Repeat bringing the other streamers to the right side of the wreath.

6. The stems of the eggs should be cut to 1¹/₂ inches (4 cm) and glued into a grouping throughout the loops of the bows. Attach the wooden spoons by inserting them between the bow and wreath and glueing in place.

Fig. 3-12
Wooden kitchen spoons form to become the focal point in this design.

RIBBON FAN WREATH

The technique for forming ribbon fans is simple! See how great combining several into one design can look (FIG. 3-13).

You will need:

☐ 3¹/₃ yards (3.2 m) of 3-inch-wide (7.5 cm) mini dot ribbon

☐ 6²/₃ yards (6 m) of 3-inch-wide (7.5 cm) stencil print ribbon

☐ One 14-inch (35 cm) straw wreath

☐ Five 3-inch (7.5 cm) wooden kitchen utensils

☐ 5 yards (4.5 m) of ³/₈-inch-wide (1 cm) heart print ribbon

Continued

Fig. 3-13
Accordion-pleated ribbon fans make quite a visual impact when all are used together.

☐ U-shaped craft pins

☐ Thirty 3-inch-long (7.5 cm) 28-gauge pieces of cloth-covered wire

☐ Hot glue gun and sticks

1. Cut the 3¹/₃ yards (3.2 m) and 6²/₃ yards (6 m) of 3-inch-wide (7.5 cm) ribbon into thirty 12-inch (30.5 cm) lengths. Accordion-pleat each of these, making ¹/₂-inch (1.3 cm) pleats. Secure one end with a length of the cloth-covered wire. Spread the untied ends open wide to form pleated half circles.

2. Form a full circle using two of the mini dot pieces and using the flat pleat ends as a glueing surface. Fit the wired ends side-by-side in the center. Be sure the outer edges match and all forms a full circle. Repeat to form a total of five full circles from the mini dot pieces.

3. Mark the wreath off into five equally spaced sections. Glue one circle at each of the five marked locations. Continue forming twenty pleated half circles with the stencil printed ribbon.

4. Using ten half circles, glue one on either side of the circles already in place. When complete, the fans should overlap slightly as they go around the wreath. Glue five in place around the outside edge of the wreath centering them between the half circles already placed. Repeat with the remaining five half circles, placing them around the inside of the wreath. At this point the entire straw wreath will be covered from the front view.

5. Glue one wooden kitchen utensil in the center of each mini dot ribbon circle on the wreath. With one yard of the ³/₈-inch-wide (1 cm) ribbon, form an eight-loop bow of 2-inch (5 cm) loops. Secure with cloth-covered wire.

6. Continue to form a total of five bows. Attach one on top of each wooden utensil by glueing in place. Following the instructions in chapter 1, attach a hanger to the back of the wreath.

COUNTRY BROOM WREATH

Tiny straw brooms form a circular pattern on this grapevine wreath. For different looks, change the materials and ribbons used here to create your own special style (FIG. 3-14).

You will need:

☐ One 10-inch (25.5 cm) straw wreath

☐ 5¹/₂ yards (5 m) of 1¹/₂-inch-wide (4 cm) country print ribbon

□ 5 yards (4.5 m) of ³/₈-inch-wide (1 cm) mini dot ribbon

□ Five 5-inch (12.5 cm) to 6-inch (15 cm) sisal brooms

□ Five berry clusters, each containing four ¹/₂-inch (1.3 cm) berries and two silk leaves

□ Hot glue gun and stick

□ 3-inch (7.5 cm) lengths of 28-gauge cloth-covered wire

□ U-shaped craft pins

1. Secure the end of the 1¹/₂-inch-wide (4 cm) ribbon to the back of the straw wreath with a craft pin. Refer to chapter 2 for the twisted ribbon technique. Cover the wreath with this ribbon method.

2. Glue the brooms to the top of the wreath, spacing them equally around the wreath. With one yard of ribbon, form a six-loop bow having 2-inch (5 cm) loops and 4-inch (10 cm) streamers. Secure with cloth-covered wire. Continue until you have a total of five bows. Glue one bow on the handle of each broom near the broom base.

3. Trim the stems of the berry clusters to ¹/₂ inch (1.3 cm) and glue one cluster near each bow on the brooms. Attach a wreath hanger as explained in chapter 1.

Fig. 3-14
Cute, tiny little brooms circle this wreath.

APPETIZER WREATH

This type of wreath is not designed to hang on the wall, but rather, to decorate your holiday or party table (FIG. 3-15). The size of the wreath should be determined by the location and the amount of appetizers you wish to serve. You will only need the most basic materials, including straight pins,

Fig. 3-15
When planning a party, this appetizer wreath would be a hit.

decorative toothpicks, and a Styrofoam wreath. The wreath in the photo uses a 14-inch (35 cm) wreath, two boxes of 50 count decorative toothpicks, and approximately fifty 1-inch (2.5 cm) straight pins.

1. Begin by forming a ring of greens around the outside and inside of the wreath. These greens will remain on the wreath as a decorative touch while the appetizers are being eaten. The pictured wreath uses purple and white kale for this purpose. Break off leaves of the kale and pin the colors alternately around the outside and inside edges of the wreath using the straight pins.

2. At this point, the top and upper sides of the wreath remain empty. Form a pattern with the foods you choose to use on the wreath so that they will alternate and completely circle the wreath. The toothpicks are inserted into the foods and then into the wreath. Guests simply remove the toothpick with the appetizer they wish, use the toothpick to eat from, and then discard it.

3. The pictured wreath used the following foods (FIG. 3-16): one bag of radishes, a small container of cherry tomatoes, a jar of green olives, a small jar of sweet pickles, and 1½ pounds of peeled, de-veined, and cooked shrimp. Of course, you may alter this list in any way you wish, but keep in mind that it is best to choose colorful foods since this wreath will be a decoration as well as a useful serving platter.

Fig. 3-16
Use elements that are in strong contrasts and color ranges.

Seasonal Wreaths

The festive nature of the four seasons and the numerous holidays we enjoy every year, makes us want to decorate our homes, doors, and offices to match the escalating moods.

~ SPRING ~

Spring is a wonderful time of year. After enduring the long winter months, we can finally open our homes up to the fresh air, bright springtime colors, and most importantly, nature. Birds arrive making nests, the grass begins to turn green, trees begin to bud, and everything has a fresh new feeling!

SPRING DOGWOOD WREATH

This lovely spring wall basket is enhanced with lace ribbon and lovely satin flowers in the freshest spring colors (FIG. 4-1).

You will need:

- ☐ One 10-inch-wide (25.5 cm) × 12-inch-tall (30.5 cm) × 2-inch-deep (5 cm) whitewashed peach flat wall basket
- ☐ 1½ yards (1.3 m) of 1-inch-wide (2.5 cm) eggshell central gathered lace
- ☐ Two stems aqua silk dogwood, each stem containing four sections of four 1½-inch-wide (4 cm) flowers
- ☐ Two stems peach silk berries, each stem containing four clusters of three ½-inch (1.3 cm) berries
- ☐ 1½ yard (1.3 m) of ¼-inch-wide (.6 cm) aqua picot edge ribbon
- ☐ 1½ yard (1.3 m) of ¼-inch-wide (.6 cm) peach picot edge ribbon
- ☐ 2-inch (5 cm) × 4-inch (10 cm) block Sahara II foam
- ☐ 1-ounce package Spanish moss

Continued

☐ U-shaped craft pins

☐ Hot glue gun and sticks

☐ 28-gauge cloth-covered wire

☐ Optional: Design Master makes a spray whitewash that will give any basket a lovely accent.

Fig. 4-1
Dogwood and silk berries adorn the side of this delightful wall basket.

1. Glue gathered lace trim around the front of the basket handle and on all four edges of the front of the basket base.

2. Insert the foam into the left side of the basket and glue in place. Completely cover the foam with Spanish moss and secure by inserting craft pins through the moss and into the foam.

3. Cut the stems of the two dogwood to 4-inch (10 cm) lengths. Gently bend one and insert into the foam so its curve follows the shape of the left side of the basket handle. Insert the second stem into the foam and then bend it forward and over the edge of the container. The dogwood blossoms will form a line along the left side of the basket.

4. Repeat the above process with the berry stems. Cut the berry stems to 4 inches (10 cm). Insert one into the foam, following the upper curve of the basket. Bend and shape the berries to fall among the dogwood blossoms. Insert the second stem into the foam and bend forward over the basket edge, mixing with the dogwood blossoms.

5. Cut the following floral pieces away from the design: two silk dogwood leaves, three dogwood blossoms, and three berries. They should be cut from the design center where they will not be noticed.

6. Glue these pieces to the right front corner of the basket.

7. Following instructions in chapter 2, form a peach bow with eight 2-inch (5 cm) loops and two 7-inch (17.5 cm) streamers . Secure the bow with a 3-inch (7.5 cm) length of cloth-covered wire and glue to the center of the basket handle. Wrap the wire ends around the handle for extra support. Repeat, forming an identical bow with the aqua ribbon and glueing into the center of the peach one.

SPRING EUCALYPTUS WREATH

The fragrant smell of fresh eucalyptus will be a welcoming aroma after the long days of winter (FIG. 4-2).

Fig. 4-2
Eucalyptus wreaths are beautiful as well as aromatic.

You will need:

☐ One 14-inch (35 cm) straw wreath

☐ 1 pound baby green eucalyptus

Continued

☐ 2 yards (1.8 m) of 2³/₄-inch-wide (7 cm) peach paper ribbon

☐ One 3-inch (7.5 cm) partridge in pastel colors

☐ One 3-inch (7.5 cm) raffia bird nest

☐ 1-ounce package preserved gypsophila

☐ Three 1-inch (2.5 cm) bird eggs

☐ One stem pink silk dogwood containing sixteen 1¹/₂-inch-wide (4 cm) flowers

☐ One stem blue silk dogwood containing sixteen 1¹/₂-inch-wide (4 cm) flowers

☐ 4 yards (3.6 m) of ⁷/₈-inch-wide (2 cm) yellow paper ribbon, untwisted

☐ 2 yards (1.8 m) of ⁷/₈-inch-wide (2 cm) blue satin ribbon

☐ ¹/₂ pound U-shaped craft pins

☐ Wired wooden picks

☐ 28-gauge cloth-covered wire

☐ Hot glue gun and sticks

1. Begin covering the inside and outside of the wreath with the larger bottom pieces of eucalyptus by pinning them down in a few places as they circle the sides of the wreath.

2. Break the remaining eucalyptus into lengths of 4 inches (10 cm) to 5 inches (12.5 cm). Hold two or three pieces together and pin to the wreath at the base of the cluster. Work around the wreath, covering the space with eucalyptus clusters. Leave 4 inches (10 cm) uncovered.

3. Cut 2³/₄-inch-wide (7 cm) paper ribbon into 6-inch (15 cm) pieces. Bring the ends of one piece together, pinch, and attach to a wired wood pick, as described in chapter 2. Continue forming six total loops. Insert these in a grouping on the bare spot of the wreath.

4. Glue the nest into the center of the loops, then glue the bird and eggs inside the nest.

5. Following instructions in chapter 2, form an eight-loop bow with 2 yards (1.8 m) of the ⁷/₈-inch-wide (2 cm) satin ribbon.

6. Repeat with the paper ribbon. Secure both with cloth-covered wire and pin the satin bow on top of the paper bow at the bottom of the wreath under the bird nest.

7. Cut 12-inch (30.5 cm) lengths of the remaining yellow paper ribbon, form into a collar bow as described in FIG. 4-22, and glue these equally spaced around the wreath.

8. Cut the heads of both colors of dogwood from their main stems and glue around the wreath between the other materials. Break off 3-inch (7.5 cm) lengths of gypsophila and glue through all the materials.

SPRING AWAKENING WREATH

A perky bird popping his head from the center of the pod reminds us of spring (FIG. 4-3).

Fig. 4-3
The cute little bird popping his head out of the pod creates an interesting look for this wreath.

You will need:

- ☐ One 14-inch (35 cm) × 9-inch (22.5 cm) heart-shaped grapevine wallpiece
- ☐ 1-ounce package pastel-painted ruscus
- ☐ 1³/₄ yards (4.5 m) of 1¹/₂-inch-wide (4 cm) pink floral ribbon
- ☐ 2 yards (1.8 m) of ⁷/₈-inch-wide (2 cm) pink floral ribbon
- ☐ Two painted bell pods approximately 2 inches (5 cm) to 2¹/₂ inches (6.5 cm) wide
- ☐ Small amount excelsior
- ☐ One 3-inch (7.5 cm) partridge
- ☐ Six ¹/₂-inch (1.3 cm) bird eggs
- ☐ 1-ounce green-painted gypsophila

Continued

☐ Two 12-inch (30.5 cm) stems preserved plumosa

☐ One chenille stem

☐ Hot glue gun and sticks

1. Break the ruscus into lengths ranging from 2 inches (5 cm) to 4 inches (10 cm), and glue around the outside edge of the wallpiece.

2. Following the instructions in chapter 2, form a bow with the 7/8-inch-wide (2 cm) ribbon having two 12-inch (30.5 cm) streamers, eight 3-inch (7.5 cm) loops, and no center loop. Attach this to the top left corner of the heart and glue streamers down into the center point of the heart.

3. Form a bow with the 1 1/2-inch-wide (4 cm) ribbon having two 6-inch (15 cm) streamers, eight 3-inch (7.5 cm) loops, and no center loop. Secure with the chenille stem and attach to the point of the heart. Break the stems off of the bell pods and glue one in the center of each bow.

4. Glue a small amount of excelsior into each bell pod. Three eggs should be glued into each bell pod and the partridge into the pod at the base of the wallpiece.

5. Break off the gypsophila in lengths ranging from 3 inches (7.5 cm) to 5 inches (12.5 cm), and glue it throughout the ruscus around the wreath, bows, and pods. The plumosa should be broken into individual pieces and glued near the gypsophila around the wreath.

Fig. 4-4
A ring of baskets alternating with a ring of bows create the appearance of the wreath.

~ SUMMER ~

The long lazy days of summer give us ample time to spend some leisure hours creating lovely wreaths to decorate our homes.

CIRCLE OF BASKETS WREATH

Tiny flat baskets make a perfect accent to the rustic look of this grapevine wreath (FIG. 4-4).

You will need:

☐ One 14-inch (35 cm) grapevine wreath

☐ One stem silk needlepoint ivy with six 7-inch (17.5 cm) ivy sprigs

☐ Three 4-inch-tall (10 cm) flat mauve baskets

☐ Three 4-inch-tall (10 cm) flat blue baskets

☐ 3 1/2 yards (3.2 m) of 3/8-inch-wide (1.3 cm) mauve and blue plaid ribbon

☐ 4 yards (3.6 m) of ³/₈-inch-wide (1.3 cm) blue heart patterned ribbon

☐ Hot glue gun and sticks

☐ 28-gauge cloth-covered wire

1. Remove the ivy sprigs from the stem and glue them circling the grapevine wreath.

2. Using the plaid ribbon on the blue baskets, glue a strip of ribbon across the top edge of the flat basket. Glue a blue strip of ribbon across the top and down both sides of the mauve baskets.

3. Glue the six baskets equally spaced around the wreath, alternating colors. Following the instructions in chapter 2, form an eight-loop bow with 1 yard (.9 m) of the plaid ribbon. The bow should have 1¹/₂-inch (4 cm) loops and 3-inch (7.5 cm) streamers. Secure them with cloth-covered wire. Repeat to form a total of three plaid and three blue heart bows. Glue one bow between each basket, alternating the colors around the wreath.

4. Following the instructions in chapter 1, attach a hanger to the back of the wreath.

SUMMER BASKET WREATH

The "nontraditional" shape of this design makes it a unique accent to enhance any wall (FIG. 4-5).

Fig. 4-5
A few sprigs of dried materials accented with silk daisies spotlight this bird.

You will need:

☐ One 10-inch-wide (25.5 cm) 12-inch-tall (30.5 cm) flat pink wall basket

☐ One stem pale pink satin daisies containing twelve 1-inch (2.5 cm) daisies

☐ One stem purple double-blossom flowers containing six sprigs of four 1-inch (2.5 cm) flowers per sprig

☐ 1 ounce Spanish moss

☐ 1 ounce German statice

☐ One 2-inch (5 cm) pink and lavender bird

☐ Hot glue gun and sticks

1. Glue the Spanish moss across the top edge of the basket base. Form a small circle of moss and glue to the upper left on the basket handle.

2. Cut the double-blossom sprigs apart so that each stem contains two flowers. Pull the daisy heads off of the main stem. Cut any silk leaves off of either flower stem and break the German statice into lengths of 2-inch (5 cm) to 3-inch (7.5 cm) pieces.

3. Begin by glueing two daisy heads and three double-blossom sprigs into the circle of Spanish moss on the handle. Glue the bird to the basket handle above the moss.

4. Glue the remaining floral pieces into the Spanish moss on the basket edge, equally spacing the pieces across the basket.

WHITEWASHED GRAPEVINE WREATH

Naturals are very evident in this design (FIG. 4-6), which sports a whitewashed finish on the grapevine wreath and is accented with drieds and lots of paper ribbon.

You will need:

☐ One 10-inch (25.5 cm) whitewashed grapevine wreath

☐ 4 yards (3.6 m) untwisted blue whitewashed paper ribbon

☐ 3½ yards (3.2 m) untwisted mauve whitewashed paper ribbon

☐ 2 yards (1.8 m) untwisted white paper ribbon

☐ 3-ounce bundle blue Florentine flowers (type of dried flower)

☐ 3-ounce bundle mauve Florentine flowers (type of dried flower)

☐ Three eggshell chenille stems

☐ 28-gauge cloth-covered wire

☐ Hot glue gun and sticks

☐ Optional: If you cannot find a whitewashed wreath, spray a natural wreath with Design Master whitewash spray.

1. Following instructions in chapter 2, untwist 1 yard (.9 m) of blue paper ribbon and form a bow with two 9-inch (22.5 cm) streamers and six 4-inch loops. Do not add a center loop. Untwist 1¹/₂ yards (1.3 m) of mauve paper ribbon and cut in half width wise, forming two pieces approximately 2 inches (5 cm) wide × 1¹/₂ yards (1.3 m) long. Using one of these pieces, form a bow with two 6-inch (15 cm) streamers and six 3-inch (7.5 cm) loops.

2. Braid together 2 yards (1.8 m) each of mauve, blue, and white paper ribbon, which has been untwisted. For instructions on braiding see chapter 2. Secure the ends with cloth-covered wire. Trim away excess wire ends, then wrap a small piece of paper ribbon over the wire. Untwist the ends of the ribbon, flaring them out.

3. Form the braid into a two-loop bow shape as shown in FIG. 4-7. Secure the center with a chenille stem and wire it into the center of the blue bow.

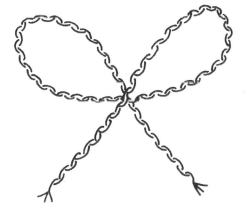

Fig. 4-6 (Above)
Braided whitewashed paper ribbon is used to accent a whitewashed wreath

Fig. 4-7 (Left)
Follow this diagram to form a braided bow to attach to the whitewashed wreath.

4. Trim away the excess chenille stem and glue the mauve bow on top of the braid in the center of the blue bow. Form the remaining 6 inches (15 cm) of blue paper ribbon into a circle. Secure the ends with a chenille stem and glue into the center of the mauve bow as its center loop. Wire the entire bow to the bottom of the wreath.

5. Form groups of four Florentine flowers. Each group should have one piece measuring 6 inches (15 cm), one piece measuring 5 inches (12.5 cm), one piece measuring 4 inches (10 cm), and one piece measuring 3

inches (7.5 cm). Glue these groups randomly around and through the loops between the blue and mauve bow. Form groups of four flowers measuring 3 inches (7.5 cm), 2 inches (5 cm), 1½ inches (4 cm), and 1 inch (2.5 cm). Repeat with other flowers until desired look is achieved.

COUNTRY MOSS WREATH

The look of country is depicted in this design (FIG. 4-8), with the Spanish moss wreath, several drieds, and a cute cotton ribbon.

Fig. 4-8
This country wreath is unique in its heart-shape form.

You will need:

- [ ] One 12-inch (30.5 cm) Spanish moss heart wreath
- [ ] 2 yards (1.8 m) of 1½-inch-wide (4 cm) country print ribbon
- [ ] Eight 12-inch (30.5 cm) stems mauve eucalyptus
- [ ] Three stems mauve protea with 2-inch-wide (5 cm) heads
- [ ] 1-ounce package German statice
- [ ] Eight 12-inch (30.5 cm) French blue ting ting stems
- [ ] Approx. 12 lagurus stems (bunny tails)

☐ Green floral tape

☐ Hot glue gun and sticks

☐ Wired wooden picks

☐ One eggshell chenille stem

☐ U-shaped craft pins

1. Form a cluster with pieces of German statice measuring in length from 6 inches (15 cm) to 8 inches (20 cm), and three 6-inch (15 cm) pieces of mauve eucalyptus. Using craft pins, pin the cluster to the center on the left side of the heart wreath.

2. Pin three 12-inch (30.5 cm) eucalyptus stems, angling them down along the left side of the wreath end-to-end with the first cluster of eucalyptus. Cut stems of statice at an angle 6 inches (15 cm) to 8 inches (20 cm) long and insert above and below the eucalyptus pieces.

3. Following instructions in chapter 2, form a bow having two 12-inch (30.5 cm) streamers and eight 3$^{1}/_{2}$-inch (8.8 cm) loops. Pin this bow over the stems of dried materials. Pinch and glue the streamers into the dried materials.

4. Break the eucalyptus into three 4-inch (10 cm) pieces and glue into the center of the bow. Break the statice into 3-inch (7.5 cm) to 4-inch (10 cm) pieces and glue throughout the bow loops.

5. Cut the protea stems to 3-inch (7.5 cm) lengths. Glue one protea into the bow center, glue the second extending up from the bow, and glue the third extending downward.

6. Bring the ends of the ting ting together to form a loop. Attach the loop to a wired wooden pick and floral-tape over the stem to secure. Repeat to form all loops. Insert these throughout the design.

7. Cut the lagurus stems to 3 inches (7.5 cm) and glue pieces between the bow loops and other floral pieces. Follow the instructions in chapter 1 for attaching a hanger to the back of the wreath.

HEART-SHAPED BABY'S BREATH WREATH

The soft look of baby's breath is used as a base for several varieties of dried materials creating a spectacular look (FIG. 4-9).

You will need:

☐ One 12-inch (30.5 cm) heart-shaped straw wreath

☐ 4-ounce bundle glittered bleached gypsophila

☐ Eight yellow Holland dried roses with 1$^{1}/_{2}$-inch-long (4 cm) heads

☐ Thirty-six pale blue-green lagurus (bunny tails)

Continued

Fig. 4-9
Several different dried
materials are combined to
create a special feeling.

☐ Approx. 24 pieces purple statice sinuata

☐ U-shaped craft pins

☐ 28-gauge cloth-covered wire

☐ Hot glue gun and sticks

1. Break the gypsophila into bunches 3 inches (7.5 cm) to 4 inches (10 cm) long. Use craft pins to attach the bunches to the wreath. Overlap the bunches as you go around the wreath to completely cover.

2. The heads of the Holland dried roses should be broken off and glued randomly around the wreath, interspersed with the lagurus and the statice heads. Continue to add materials until a nice full feeling is achieved.

3. Following instructions in chapter 1, attach a hanger to the back of the wreath.

~ FALL ~

The crisp feeling in the air tells us when fall is approaching. The beauty of the fall leaves entice us to use these same rich colors to decorate our doors and homes.

The kitchen is the heart of family life. These designs accent the warm feeling of a kitchen, as well as incorporate several items only found in a kitchen.

The natural charm of the brick fireplace is repeated in all of the wreath designs highlighted here.

Bright colors, funny faces, and cuddly teddy bears work to create a whimsical atmosphere for children.

The teal and green used in these designs are beautiful when accented with either peach or pink. Open, airy feelings are evoked.

Christmas is a special time when we like to give parties and remember family and friends. Wreaths to decorate our homes or give as gifts are extremely popular.

Antique Chinese doors are used as a backdrop for the spectacular feather wreath. Any of the designs shown can be used in any foyer, den, or office.

A soft, romantic mood is created in this room with the display of several lush-looking wreaths complete with feathers, pearls, potpourri, and candles.

The look of spring pops through with the bright, perky colors used in these designs. Little Lamsy Divy, shown in the center, would delight any child.

Any family member will be delighted when they receive this wreath spotlighting all of their favorite little people.

Choose colors and materials that
accent the decor of the room. Here,
deep, rich colors add a masculine
feeling.

Romantic-styled wreaths are
especially appealing because they
are soft in appearance.

Fall is a wonderful time of year when we bring the colors we see outside into our homes.

The deep, rich shades of peach are very popular in today's home decor.

DECORATIVE DOOR BOW

Paper ribbon is used as a background for the grapevine wreath and berries used in this design (FIG. 4-10).

You will need:

- [ ] 3 yards (2.7 m) of 3¹/₂-inch-wide (8.8 cm) peach paper ribbon
- [ ] One 7-inch (17.5 cm) heart-shaped grapevine wreath
- [ ] Two 6-inch-long (15 cm) berry and cone clusters
- [ ] 1-ounce package peach glittered gypsophila
- [ ] Hot glue gun and sticks
- [ ] 28-gauge cloth-covered wire

1. If the paper ribbon is purchased twisted in a coil, untwist before use. The easiest way is to soak the paper first for a few minutes in warm water, then untwist.

2. Following the instructions in chapter 2, form a six-loop bow without a center loop, having 6-inch (15 cm) loops and two 14-inch (35 cm) streamers. Secure with the cloth-covered wire, forming the wire ends into a hook to hang the bow.

3. Glue the heart into the center of the bow with the bottom point of the heart falling in front of the center of the bow.

4. Cut the berry and cone cluster stems so ¹/₂ inch (1.3 cm) of stem remains. Slightly curve the stems. Glue one cluster along the left side of the heart and the second cascading below the heart end-to-end with the first stem. The entire line of berries should resemble an S-curve.

5. Break off 2-inch (5 cm) to 3-inch (7.5 cm) lengths of gypsophila and glue throughout the berries, cones, and pods until the desired fullness is achieved.

Fig. 4-10
In this design, the bow is the main feature, which is then accented by the wreath and berries.

CINNAMON BROOM

Cinnamon-scented products are new and exciting. Should you be unable to find them, simply scent your broom or wreath using a few drops of cinnamon oil, available in the potpourri section of your local store, or use Design Master's cinnamon-scented spray when the design is complete (FIG. 4-11).

You will need:

- [ ] One 12-inch (30.5 cm) cinnamon-scented broom
- [ ] 2 yards (1.8 m) of ⁷/₈-inch-wide (2 cm) rust plaid ribbon

Continued

Fig. 4-11
Cinnamon brooms add a wonderful fall aroma to the air.

- ☐ 2 yards (1.8 m) of 1¹/₂-inch-wide (4 cm) peach gauze-like ribbon
- ☐ Five 3-inch (7.5 cm) preserved apple slices. (If you wish to preserve your own apples, see the "Preserved Apples" section in chapter 3.)
- ☐ Six 4-inch (10 cm) preserved oak leaves
- ☐ 1-ounce package German statice
- ☐ 28-gauge cloth-covered wire
- ☐ Hot glue gun and sticks

1. Following instructions in chapter 2, take the 1¹/₂-inch-wide (4 cm) ribbon and form an eight-loop bow with 4-inch (10 cm) loops, no center loop, and two 6-inch (15 cm) streamers. Secure the bow with cloth-covered wire and glue to the front of the broom.

2. With the rust plaid ribbon, form a second bow having eight 3-inch (7.5 cm) loops and two 6-inch (15 cm) streamers. Also secure this bow with cloth-covered wire and glue into the center of the first bow.

3. Glue the five apple slices into the bow loops in a circular fashion. The oak leaves should be glued around the bow loops and apple slices. Fill between all with 2-inch (5 cm) to 3-inch (7.5 cm) pieces of German statice.

DOUBLE FALL GRAPEVINE WREATH

Using two wreaths in combination together creates an exciting visual effect (FIG. 4-12).

Fig. 4-12
For extra interest, wire two grapevine wreaths together.

You will need:

☐ One 14-inch (35 cm) grapevine wreath

☐ One 8-inch (20 cm) grapevine wreath

☐ Two 15-inch (38 cm) oak leaf branches

☐ Two 12-inch (30.5 cm) berry stems, each containing fifteen 1-inch (2.5 cm) berries

☐ 2½ yards (2.3 m) of 1½-inch-wide (4 cm) orange plaid ribbon

☐ 2 yards (1.8 m) of ⅞-inch-wide (2 cm) fall print ribbon

☐ Hot glue gun and sticks

☐ 28-gauge cloth-covered wire

1. Place the 8-inch (20 cm) wreath on top of the left side of the 14-inch (35 cm) wreath. Glue the two wreaths together and wrap with cloth-covered wire for extra security.

2. Lay one berry stem on top of one leaf stem. Trim stems to 2 inches (5 cm) and wire the two stems together. Repeat with second branch and berry stem. Place the two wired sections together end-to-end over the joining location of the small and large wreath.

3. Following the instructions in chapter 2 and using the 1½-inch-wide (4 cm) ribbon, form an eight-loop bow, with each loop being 4 inches (10 cm) long and two streamers being 12 inches (30.5 cm) long. Secure with wire, then glue to the wreath at the point where the two stem ends join.

4. Using the ⅞-inch-wide (2 cm) ribbon, form a second bow with eight 2½-inch (6.5 cm) loops and two 12-inch (30.5 cm) streamers. Secure with wire and glue into the center of the first bow.

5. Following instructions in chapter 1, attach a hanger to the back of the wreath.

FALL DEER WREATH

The traditional look of fall is evoked in rustic grapevine wreath, accented with an elegant deer (FIG. 4-13).

Fig. 4-13
The deer nestled into the center of this design is quite pleasing.

You will need:

☐ One 16-inch (40.5 cm) grapevine wreath

☐ One 5-inch (12.5 cm) flocked sitting deer

☐ 2½ yards (2.3 m) of 2-inch-wide (5 cm) French blue untwisted paper ribbon

☐ 1½ yards (1.3 m) of 2-inch-wide (5 cm) blue whitewashed untwisted paper ribbon

☐ Three 10-inch (25.5 cm) pine stems

☐ Three 7-inch (17.5 cm) berry and cone stems

☐ 1-ounce package Spanish moss

☐ One chenille stem

☐ Hot glue gun and sticks

☐ Optional: Spray the grapevine wreath with Glossy Wood Tone from Design Master. This product accents and highlights the beauty of the grapevine.

1. Glue the moss into the center bottom of the wreath. Attach the deer by glueing him into the center of the moss. Also allow some glue to adhere the deer directly to the wreath.

2. Following the instructions in chapter 2 and using the blue paper ribbon, form a bow with two 10-inch (25.5 cm) streamers and six 5-inch (12.5 cm) loops. There should not be a center loop on this bow. Secure the bow with one-half of the chenille stem.

3. Using the whitewashed ribbon, form a second bow with two 10-inch (25.5 cm) streamers and four 3½-inch (8.8 cm) loops . Secure this bow with the other half of the chenille stem and glue it on top of the first bow. Attach this double bow to the bottom of the wreath under the deer.

4. Cut all pine and berry stems to ½ inch (1.3 m). Glue one pine stem at the center top of the wreath. Glue one berry stem in the center of the pine stem.

5. Repeat by glueing one pine stem on either side of the bow and one berry stem into the middle of each of these pine stems. Attach a wreath hanger to the back.

Fig. 4-14
Spooky ghosts and creepy bats—perfect for Halloween!

HALLOWEEN GHOST WREATH

Spooky ghosts and scary bats adorn this Halloween wreath, designed to delight young and old alike (FIG. 4-14).

You will need:

☐ One 12-inch (30.5 cm) straw wreath

☐ 6 yards (5.4 m) of 1¹/2-inch-wide (4 cm) Halloween print ribbon

☐ One 6-inch-wide (15 cm) × 5-inch-tall (12.5 cm) wooden gate

☐ Three 2¹/2-inch-tall (6.5 cm) ghost picks

☐ Two 4-inch-wide (10 cm) bat picks

☐ Six 3¹/2-inch-long (8.8 cm) silk fall oak leaves

☐ Three 1-inch (2.5 cm) flocked pumpkins

☐ Hot glue guns and sticks

☐ U-shaped craft pins

1. Secure the end of the ribbon to the back of the wreath with a craft pin. Wrap the ribbon around to the front of the wreath. Hold the ribbon snugly in the center of the top of the wreath with your thumb. Twist the ribbon a complete turn until the right side is again facing up. Again wrap the ribbon around the back of the wreath to the front and repeat the twisting step. Continue in this fashion until the wreath is completely covered securing the other end with a craft pin. (See chapter 2 for additional information on the twisted-ribbon technique.)

2. Glue the gate to the bottom front of the wreath. Remove the picks from the bats, ghosts, and pumpkins. Glue the two bats side-by-side on the upper left of the wreath. Attach two ghosts to the front of the gate on the right-hand side and one on the left side.

3. The three pumpkins should be glued to the top of the gate. Attach two oak leaves to the upper right of the wreath and two more on either side of the gate behind the ghosts. Follow the instructions in chapter 1 to attach a hanger to the back of the wreath.

Fig. 4-15
This fall wreath can be created very quickly because of the use of pre-made materials.

HALLOWEEN SCARECROW WREATH

Rich fall tones and a cute scarecrow figure work together to create this easy-to-make Halloween wreath (FIG. 4-15).

You will need:

☐ One 12-inch (30.5 cm) straw wreath

☐ 2¹/2 yards (2.3 m) of 1¹/2-inch-wide (4 cm) yellow country print ribbon

☐ 2¹/2 yards (2.3 m) of 1¹/2-inch-wide (4 cm) orange fall print ribbon

☐ One 8-inch (20 cm) scarecrow figurine

☐ Two 2¹/2-inch (6.5 cm) lacquered pumpkins on stems

☐ Eight 3-inch (7.5 cm) silk fall leaves

☐ Hot glue gun and sticks

☐ U-shaped craft pins

1. Using the yellow ribbon, spiral-wrap the wreath, securing the ends with craft pins. Wrap the wreath in the opposite direction with the orange ribbon, again securing the ends with craft pins.

2. Glue the scarecrow to the inside center of the wreath. Cut the pumpkin stems to ¹/₂ inch (1.3 cm) and insert one on either side of the figurine.

3. Pull the fall leaves off of the stem and glue each individually into a cluster under the scarecrow and pumpkins. Attach hanger to the back of the wreath following instructions in chapter 1.

～ WINTER/CHRISTMAS ～

This is the time of year where we all prepare our homes for a wonderful season of sharing. We want wreaths on our walls, garlands on our mantles, and bows on our trees—all to create a festive, warm feeling among family and friends.

"DECK THE HALLS" WREATH

This unique wreath design features a decorated Christmas tree in its center, creating a new twist on this popular holiday motif (FIG. 4-16).
    You will need:

☐ One 14-inch (35 cm) grapevine wreath

☐ 3 yards (2.7 m) of 1¹/₂-inch-wide (4 cm) red-striped ribbon

☐ 2¹/₂ yards (2.3 m) of 1¹/₂-inch-wide (4 cm) white-striped ribbon

☐ One 12-inch (30.5 cm) tabletop tree

☐ Twenty-four ¹/₂-inch-wide (1.3 cm) red glass balls

☐ Twelve 1-inch-wide (2.5 cm) jingle bells with tiny bow

☐ Twelve 1-inch-wide (2.5 cm) premade 2-loop red bows

☐ 1 yard (.9 m) gold thread for tree garland

☐ Two silk holly picks with four 4-inch (10 cm) leaves and twelve ¹/₂-inch (1.3 cm) red berries

☐ Twelve 1-inch (2.5 cm) packages

☐ One chenille stem

☐ Hot glue gun and sticks

Fig. 4-16
A miniature Christmas tree highlights the center of this wreath.

1. First, wrap the wreath with 3 yards (2.7 m) of the red striped ribbon and secure the ends by glueing them in place.

2. Attach the glass balls, bows, and bells to the branches of the tree, and swag the gold garland around the tree. Glue the decorated tree into the center of the wreath.

3. Following instructions in chapter 2 and using 1¹/₂-inch (4 cm) white striped ribbon, form a bow that has eight 3¹/₂-inch (8.8 cm) loops and two 12-inch (30.5 cm) streamers. Secure the bow with a chenille stem and glue at the base in front of the tree.

4. Cut the stems of one holly pick to ¹/₂ inch (1.3 m). Spread the leaves and berries out and glue to the upper-left corner of the wreath. Cut the other holly in half, and glue one half on either side of the bow at the wreath base.

5. The stems of the packages should be cut to approximately 4 inches (10 cm) and glued throughout the bow loops.

PINECONE CANDY CANE

This cane-shaped wallpiece is a delightful change from the traditional circular wreath design (FIG.4-17).

You will need:

□ One 11-inch (28 cm) wire candy cane form

□ Eleven 2-inch (5 cm) pinecones

□ Seven 2-inch (5 cm) sprigs of pine, each having one ³/₈-inch-wide (.8 cm) red berry

□ 2 yards (1.8 m) of ⁵/₈-inch-wide (1.5 cm) red plaid ribbon

□ 28-gauge cloth-covered wire

□ Hot glue gun and sticks

□ One 3-inch (7.5 cm) chenille stem

Fig. 4-17
The candy cane shape of this wallpiece is quite unique.

1. Glue the pinecones onto the wire frame. If more support is needed to glue the cones to the frame, wrap the wire frame first with 3-inch (7.5 cm) strips of garbage bags. Let dry completely. Wrap the cane with 1 yard (.9 m) of ribbon, glueing the ends to secure.

2. Cut the stems off of the pine sprigs and glue alternately on the right and left side of the cones.

3. Following instructions in chapter 2, form a bow with six 2¹/₂-inch (6.5 cm) loops and two 5-inch (12.5 cm) streamers. Secure this bow to the side of the cane with 28-gauge wire.

MARCH INTO CHRISTMAS WREATH

Whimsical describes this delightful design, complete with a toy soldier and artificial candy and treats (FIG. 4-18).

You will need:

☐ One 16-inch (40.5 cm) pine wreath

☐ One 10-inch-tall (25.5 cm) soldier figurine

☐ 3 yards (2.7 m) of 1¹/₂-inch-wide (4 cm) plaid ribbon

☐ Ten 4-inch (10 cm) candy canes

☐ Six candy picks containing four to six 2-inch (5 cm) pieces of candy

☐ Four 5-inch-tall (12.5 cm) suckers

☐ One chenille stem

☐ Hot glue gun and sticks

Fig. 4-18
Although the soldier in this design is dominant, interest is also placed with the candy tucked around the pine wreath.

1. Glue the toy soldier into the center of the pine wreath. Following instructions in chapter 2, form a bow with eighteen 2¹/₂-inch (6.5 cm) loops and two 6-inch (15 cm) streamers and attach it at the base of the wreath with the chenille stem.

2. Glue the canes equally spaced around the wreath using two together at each location. The candy picks should also be equally spaced around the wreath between the candy canes previously placed.

3. Glue two suckers on either side of the soldier figurine.

MERRY CHRISTMAS WREATH

This inexpensive wreath is a wonderful gift item at Christmas. Change some of the colors and materials used to create a delightful new look each time (FIG. 4-19).

You will need:

☐ One 12-inch (30.5 cm) straw wreath

☐ 6 yards (5.4 m) of 1½-inch-wide (5 cm) red velvet ribbon

☐ 6½ yards (6 m) of 1½-inch-wide (4 cm) gold striped ribbon

☐ 3 yards (2.7 m) of ¼-inch-wide (.6 cm) red double-face satin ribbon with gold edging

☐ 3½ yards (3.2 m) of ¼-inch-wide (.6 cm) red double-face satin ribbon

☐ Five ½-inch (1.3 cm) gold jingle bells

☐ 6-inch (15 cm) tabletop tree

☐ Twelve 1½-inch-wide (4 cm) two-loop premade bows

☐ Twelve ½-inch-wide (1.3 cm) mini gold cowbells

☐ One 5-inch-wide (12.5 cm) wooden painted "Merry Christmas" sign

☐ Two 3-inch (7.5 cm) mini decorated stockings

☐ Eight ½-inch (1.3 cm) packages of picks

☐ Six 4-inch (10 cm) candy canes

☐ 28-gauge cloth-covered wire

☐ U-shaped craft pins

☐ Hot glue gun and sticks

Fig. 4-19
A tiny tree and stockings filled with goodies—what more could we want at Christmas time.

1. Completely wrap the wreath with 6 yards (5.4 m) of the red velvet ribbon, using craft pins to secure ends. Using 2½ yards (2.3 m) of the gold striped ribbon, spiral-wrap the wreath in one direction, securing the ends with craft pins. Repeat wrapping in the opposite direction with 2 ½ yards (2.3 m) of gold ribbon, forming an X design with the ribbon.

2. Following instructions in chapter 2, form a bow with the gold striped ribbon that has 12-inch (30.5 cm) streamers and ten 3-inch (7.5 cm) loops. Secure with cloth-covered wire and attach to the bottom of the wreath.

3. With ¼-inch-wide (.6 cm) red satin ribbon, form a second bow having sixteen 2-inch (5 cm) loops and two 12-inch (30.5 cm) streamers. Secure with a 6-inch (15 cm) length of cloth-covered wire. Cut three 10-inch (25.5 cm) lengths of ribbon and one 8-inch (20 cm) length. Hold all ends together and wire these into the back of the bow.

4. Attach this second bow on top of the first one at the base of the wreath. String the gold jingle bells onto the streamers of the narrow ribbon and tie in knots so they do not fall off.

5. Glue the miniature bows and cowbells to the tree and glue the tree onto the inside bottom of the wreath. Attach the wooden piece onto the top center of the wreath.

6. Place one stocking on either side of the wreath and fill one with packages and the other with the candy canes. Follow instructions in chapter 1 and attach a hanger to the back of the wreath.

TRIPLE CARDINAL BASKET WALLPIECE

The unusual shape of these three hearts together create a special visual effect for the holidays (FIG. 4-20).

Fig. 4-20
The beauty of this triple heart design is accented with tiny pieces of Christmas greens and birds.

You will need:

☐ One 20-inch (50.5 cm) triple grapevine heart wallpiece
☐ Eight 4-inch (10 cm) frosted cedar picks
☐ Three 6-inch (15 cm) holly and berry picks
☐ Three 5-inch (12.5 cm) red cardinals
☐ 1 yard (.9 m) of $^1/_8$-inch-wide (.3 cm) red double-face satin ribbon
☐ 28-gauge cloth-covered wire
☐ Hot glue gun and sticks

1. Cut the stems of two cedar picks and one holly and berry pick to 1 inch (2.5 cm) and glue them onto the top left-hand corner of the first heart. Repeat on the right curve of the third heart.

2. Glue one cardinal into the center top of the first heart. Cut the remaining cedar and berry picks to 1 inch (2.5 cm) and glue them into the bottom center point of the heart. They should be glued along the inside edges of the basket.

3. The two remaining cardinals should be glued into the center heart. Use the double-face satin ribbon to swag between birds, glueing to each bird beak.

HOLIDAY BOW WREATH

Full tufts of ribbon add a festive look to this design. Different styles, colors, and patterns of ribbon are used to add contrast and color changes (FIG. 4-21).

You will need:

☐ One 14-inch (35 cm) straw wreath

☐ 10 yards (9 m) of 1¹/₂-inch-wide (4 cm) red satin ribbon

☐ 10 yards (9 m) of 1¹/₂-inch-wide (4 cm) gold striped ribbon

☐ 10 yards (9 m) of 1¹/₂-inch-wide (4 cm) Christmas print ribbon

☐ ¹/₂ pound U-shaped craft pins

1. Cut all the ribbon into 18-inch (45.5 cm) pieces. Form each piece into a bow following the diagram in FIG. 4-22. Place a craft pin over the pinched portion of the bow and insert the pin into the wreath to secure the bow to the wreath. Fluff out the loops and streamers for a full look.

Fig. 4-21 (Above) Lots and lots of ribbon loops in a multitude of colors and textures.

Fig. 4-22 (Right) Fold your ribbon as shown here to form tiny collar bows.

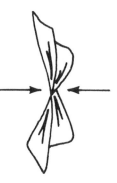

2. Continue making bows and inserting them into the wreath. Have the bows turned in different directions so they fill in the spaces on the wreath. Alternate the patterns of ribbon as you go through the wreath.

3. Attach a wreath hanger following instructions in chapter 1.

PINECONE RIBBON WREATH VARIATION

This variation of the ribbon wreath above adds a wonderful texture change by including pinecones (FIG. 4-23).

To make, simply eliminate several rows of bows from the inside center and top of the wreath and replace them with pinecones and other miniature pods.

You will use approximately fifty 2-inch (5 cm) pinecones and pods, and will be eliminating approximately 3 yards (33.7 m) of each type of ribbon.

The cones and pods should be hot glued to the wreath base.

Fig. 4-23
Use pinecones around the center of the wreath surrounded by ribbon loops for a festive touch.

Wreaths for Children

*B*right colors, teddy bears, and whimsical faces all go together to create delightful wreaths for children. In the first project, children can spotlight their creativity by tracing their hands, cutting them out, and forming them into a ringed wreath for all to see.

RING OF HANDS WREATH

This wreath can be designed by one child using his or her hand over and over again, or several children can participate—each tracing his or her own hand, labeling it with his or her name, and decorating the wreath after it has been constructed (FIG. 5-1).

Fig. 5-1
Children's hands create a very unique wreath.

You will need:

☐ One 14-inch (35 cm) flat Styrofoam wreath

☐ 6 yards (5.4 m) red satin ribbon

☐ Approx. 8 sheets of 9-inch (22.5 cm) × 12-inch (30.5 cm) bright-colored paper

☐ White craft glue

☐ Pencil

☐ Straight pins

☐ U-shaped craft pin

1. Completely wrap the wreath with the red satin ribbon, pinning the ends to secure. Have the children measure their hands with the pencil and cut each one out. The wreath pictured used 16 hands around the wreath. You may need more or less depending on the sizes of the children's hands.

2. Glue the hands around the wreath, angling them slightly left, then right around the wreath. If several children's hands are used, have each one sign their name to identify their hand.

LITTLE LAMSY DIVY

This perky lamb's face will delight any child as it adorns his bedroom wall (FIG. 5-2).

You will need:

☐ One 12-inch (30.5 cm) wicker hat

  ☐ One 9-inch (22.5 cm) × 12-inch (30.5 cm) sheet brown felt

  ☐ One 9-inch (22.5 cm) × 12-inch (30.5 cm) sheet beige felt

  ☐ One 9-inch (22.5 cm) × 12-inch (30.5 cm) sheet deep pink felt

  ☐ Small amount polyester stuffing material

☐ 5 yards (4.5 m) of 2-inch-wide (5 cm) blue and mauve gingham ribbon

☐ One stem pink daisies containing ten 2-inch (5 cm) flowers

  ☐ One stem blue double blossoms containing six sprigs of four 1-inch (5 cm) flowers

  ☐ Two 1-inch (5 cm) movable eyes

☐ Brown acrylic paint

☐ Beige acrylic paint

☐ Sponge brush

☐ White craft glue

Fig. 5-2
Little Lamsy Divy is a perky addition to a child's wall.

□ Hot glue gun and sticks
□ Two eggshell chenille stems
□ One deep pink chenille stem

1. Paint the crown of the hat with brown acrylic paint. Paint the brim of the hat with beige acrylic paint. Cut the ears from the beige and brown felt following the diagrams in FIG. 5-3.

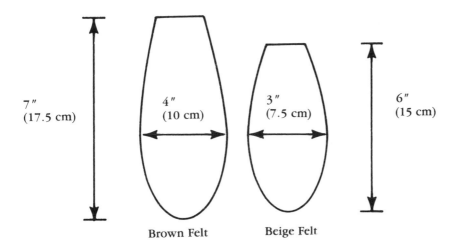

7"
(17.5 cm)

4"
(10 cm)

3"
(7.5 cm)

6"
(15 cm)

Brown Felt   Beige Felt

Fig. 5-3
Trace the lamb's ears from felt.

2. Glue the beige car on top of the brown ear. Pinch at the top and glue together. Gluc the felt pieces to the sides of the hat crown for ears. Fluff out the polyester stuffing and glue to the top of the crown of the hat.

3. Following the instructions in chapter 2 and using 1½ yards (1.3 m) of ribbon, form a tailored bow and glue to the top of the head. Form three loops of ribbon, one measuring 12 inches (30.5 cm), one measuring 10 inches (25.5 cm), and the last measuring 8 inches (20 cm). Glue these loops under the chin as streamers. With the remainder of the ribbon, form a tailored bow and glue on top of the loop ends under the chin. Slightly pull the bow loops apart to fill in space.

4. Glue the eyes to the lamb face. Cut two 1½-inch (4 cm) circles from the deep pink felt and glue on as cheeks. Form one-half of the deep pink chenille stem into a mouth by bending it in half (FIG. 5-4, left). Twist the chenille stem together 1 inch (5 cm) below the fold (FIG. 5-4, middle). Bring the ends of the chenille stem up to form a smile (FIG. 5-4, right). Glue the smile to the face of the lamb.

Fig. 5-4
Left: For the mouth, first bend the chenille stem in half. Middle: Twist the chenille stem 1 inch (2.5 cm) from the fold. Right: Bend the ends of the chenille stem up to form a smile.

TEDDY BEAR STEPLADDER WREATH

These whimsical bears appear as though they are actually climbing the ladder. This design makes for a wonderful conversation piece or a perfect opening for a bedtime story (FIG. 5-5).

You will need:

- One 12-inch (30.5 cm) straw wreath
- 7 yards (6.3 m) red satin ribbon
- 8 yards (7.2 m) yellow gingham ribbon
- One 12-inch (30.5 cm) red wooden ladder
- Two 4-inch (10 cm) teddy bears
- Assorted color felt squares
- Three 1-inch (2.5 cm) wooden blocks
- Hot glue gun and sticks
- Straight pins
- 28-gauge cloth-covered wire

1. Completely wrap the wreath with 6 yards (5.4 m) of red satin ribbon, pinning ends to secure. Following the instructions in chapter 2 and using 6 yards (5.4 m) of the yellow gingham ribbon, perform the twisted ribbon technique around the wreath.

2. Following the instructions in chapter 2, form a layered bow. The bottom layer should be made out of the yellow gingham ribbon, with eight 3-inch (7.5 cm) loops and 6-inch (15 cm) streamers. The top bow is formed with six 2-inch (5 cm) loops and 4- inch (10 cm) streamers. Attach the bow to the lower left side of the wreath.

3. Glue the wooden ladder angling up the center of the wreath. Glue the teddy bears to the rungs of the ladder. Following the outlines in FIG. 5-6, cut out felt letters and glue along the wreath and into the bears' hands.

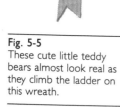

Fig. 5-5
These cute little teddy bears almost look real as they climb the ladder on this wreath.

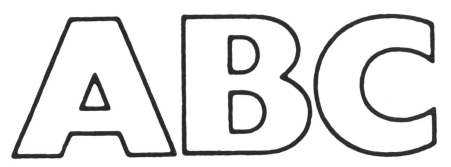

Fig. 5-6
Trace these letters onto different colors of felt to attach to the wreath.

SAM THE CLOWN WALLPIECE

Bright primary colors in rainbow tones were used to create this funny clown face (FIG. 5-7).

You will need:

☐ One 16-inch (40.5 cm) flat Styrofoam wreath

☐ ½ yard (.5 m) of muslin fabric or an 18-inch (45.5 cm) square sheet of white paper

☐ 9 yards (8.1 m) of 1-inch-wide (2.5 cm) rainbow ribbon

☐ 18 yards (16.2 m) of ⁵/₈-inch-wide (1.5 cm) rainbow ribbon

☐ 3 yards (2.7 m) of 3-inch-wide (7.5 cm) red shiny ribbon or glossy paper

Continued

Fig. 5-7
Sam, the funny-face clown, will delight any child.

- [ ] One 2-inch (5 cm) red pom-pom
- [ ] One sheet yellow felt
- [ ] One sheet red felt
- [ ] One sheet blue felt
- [ ] One sheet purple felt
- [ ] 28-gauge cloth-covered wire
- [ ] White craft glue
- [ ] Straight pins
- [ ] Stapler and staples

1. Completely wrap the wreath with the 1-inch (2.5 cm) rainbow ribbon, pinning ends to secure. Pin the muslin fabric or white paper securely to the back of the wreath. Trim away the excess material around the outside edge of the circular wreath.

2. Following the instructions in chapter 2 and using 1 yard (.9 m) of 5/8-inch (1.5 cm) ribbon, form a basic bow with 1 1/2-inch-long (4 cm). Continue forming a total of 18 bows. Pin and glue the bows around the top half of the wreath as hair for the clown.

3. Following the diagram in FIG. 6-10, use 1 1/2 yards (1.3 m) of the red ribbon or paper and box-pleat the length of ribbon with 1-inch (2.5 cm) pleats. Repeat to form a second length of box-pleated ribbon. Pin one row of box-pleated ribbon around the bottom half of the wreath between the hair bows. Pin the second row 1/2 inch (1.3 cm) above the first row.

4. Following diagrams in FIGS. 5-8, 5-9, and 5-10, cut the items from the indicated pieces of felt and glue to the clown's face. Glue the pom-pom nose on with the felt pieces to complete the face.

Fig. 5-8
Cut Sam's mouth from yellow felt.

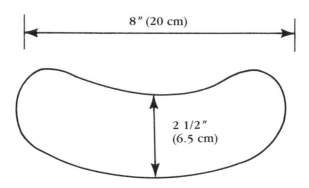

8" (20 cm)

2 1/2"
(6.5 cm)

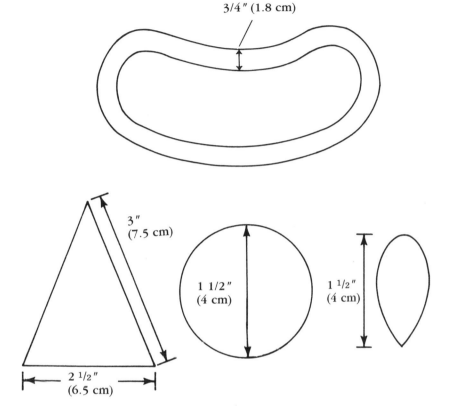

3/4 " (1.8 cm)

3 "
(7.5 cm)

2 1/2 "
(6.5 cm)

1 1/2 "
(4 cm)

1 1/2 "
(4 cm)

Fig. 5-9
Sam's lips should be cut
from red felt and glued on
top of the mouth piece.

Fig. 5-10
Left: The eye patches are
cut from yellow felt. Middle:
Eyes are cut from blue felt
and glued on top of the
patches. Right: The wide-
eyed look is achieved with
these tall eyebrows cut from
purple.

HOT AIR BALLOON BEARS

This whimsical decoration is perfect for a young child's room. The balloons are very dimensional and certainly eye-catching. Mix or match the colors to create a piece perfect for your child. The Hot Air Balloons can be created individually and hung separately from the ceiling, as in FIG. 5-11, or can be combined into a delightful mobile (see FIG. 5-15).

Single Hot Air Balloon

When choosing colors, try to have all coordinate together. If this is a gift for a baby shower and the sex of the baby is not known, use all the pastel colors to give the piece a cheery look.

You will need:

☐ One 6-inch (15 cm) Styrofoam ball

☐ 2 yards (1.8 m) of 1¹/₂-inch-wide (4 cm) solid color ribbon

Continued

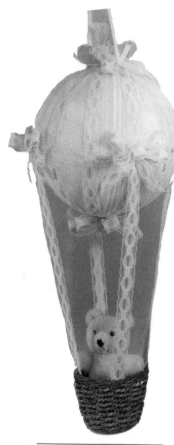

Fig. 5-11
The Hot Air Balloons can also be made individually and hung.

☐ 2 yards (1.8 m) of 1¹/₂-inch-wide (4 cm) print ribbon of coordinating color

☐ 15¹/₂ yards (13.9 m) of ¹/₂-inch-wide (1.3 cm) lacedge ribbon in a coordinating color

☐ One 3-inch-wide (7.5 cm) × 4-inch-tall (10 cm) basket

☐ One 4-inch (10 cm) teddy bear

☐ Straight pins

☐ Hot glue gun and sticks

☐ White craft glue

☐ 28-gauge cloth-covered wire

1. Cut the two 1¹/₂-inch-wide (4 cm) ribbons into 9-inch (22.5 cm) lengths. Fold each piece in half width wise, making it 9 inches (22.5 cm) × ³/₄ inch (1.6 cm). Cut both ends at an angle as in FIG. 5-12.

2. Pin the ends of six pieces of the solid color ribbon into the top end of the ball as seen in FIG. 5-13. Bring the other ends of the ribbon around the ball, equally spacing them, and pin all together at the bottom of the ball.

3. Repeat this process with the print ribbon, placing it in the spaces between the first set of ribbons. Pin and glue lengths of the lacedge ribbon over the edges of the two ribbons where they overlap to hide the cut edges.

4. Pin a length of ribbon around the center of the ball as shown in FIG. 5-14. Cut four 10-inch (25.5 cm) lengths of lacedge ribbon. These are the pieces that will attach the balloon to the basket. Glue one end of each of the four pieces equally spaced around the inside top edge of the basket. Pin the other ends of these four pieces, equally spaced around the center of the ball, onto the ribbon placed in FIG. 5-14.

5. Using the remaining lacedge ribbon, form tiny bows and attach one over each spot where the streamers meet the center of the ball. Place one bow on top of the ball and one bow on the bottom of the ball. Insert the teddy bear inside the basket and hang the balloon either with a length of ribbon or a piece of monofilament thread.

Hot Air Balloon Mobile

Group the little bears together in a mobile for three times the fun.
You will need:

☐ Three completed Hot Air Balloons as described above

☐ One 18-inch (45.5 cm) straw wreath

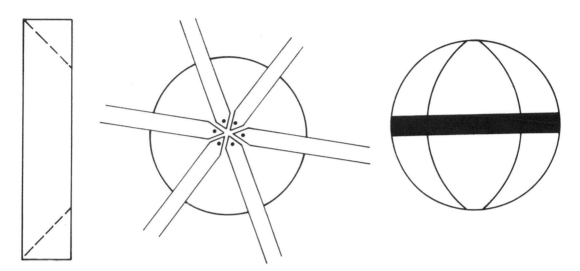

☐ 8 yards (7.2 m) of 3-inch-wide (7.5 cm) white floral print cotton ribbon

☐ 1¹/₂ yards (1.3 m) of 2¹/₂-inch-wide (6.5 cm) pink gathered lace

☐ 1¹/₂ yards (1.3 m) of 2¹/₂-inch-wide (6.5 cm) yellow gathered lace

☐ 1¹/₂ yards (1.3 m) of 2¹/₂-inch-wide (6.5 cm) blue gathered lace

☐ 3 yards (2.7 m) of 3-inch-wide (7.5 cm) lacedge pink gingham ribbon

☐ 2 yards (1.8 m) of 3-inch-wide (7.5 cm) lacedge blue gingham ribbon

☐ Straight pins

☐ White craft glue

☐ One white chenille stem

☐ 28-gauge cloth-covered wire

☐ *Note:* You will need an additional ¹/₂ yard of the narrow ribbon used on each Hot Air Balloon to hang the balloon from the wreath.

Fig. 5-12 (Above Left) Cut both ends of the ribbon at an angle.

Fig. 5-13 (Above Middle) Pin the ends of the ribbons into the top end of the ball.

Fig. 5-14 (Above Right) Pin a length of ribbon around the center of the ball.

1. Completely wrap the wreath with the white floral print cotton ribbon, pinning the ends to secure. Wreath will hang horizontally, so pin lace around edges so that it can be viewed from below. Begin by pinning blue lace around the center on the outside of the wreath. Pin the yellow row slightly above the blue and the pink just above the yellow.

2. Form a bow with the blue gingham ribbon, securing with the chenille stem. Using the pink gingham ribbon, cut three 1-yard (.9 m) pieces. *Note:* This length is approximate—each wreath will vary since each person making the wreath will be hanging it in a different location.

3. Pin one end of each of the ribbons equally spaced around the inside center of the wreath. Dip each pin in glue before inserting it into the wreath to prevent it from pulling out.

4. Gather the other ends of the three ribbons together and measure the length. Adapt or change length as needed. Use the cloth-covered wire to secure and add some glue over joining location for extra protection.

5. Wire the blue bow over the joining location.

6. Hang the three balloons using the matching ribbons. They can all be hung at the same level, or hung from different levels for interest.

Fig. 5-15
A mobile created from ribbon, Hot Air Balloons will draw a great deal of attention.

Romantic Wreaths

Soft, romantic looks are becoming a main force in home decorating for the upcoming years. Many of today's homes are decorated with large floral prints, rich color tones, delicate open-weave laces, satins, pearls, and potpourri. In this chapter you will find many ideas for wreaths that evoke this romantic look. Colors, ribbons, and accents can be changed to make your design fit the decor of the room.

NATURAL FEATHER WREATH

The natural color of the willow wreath in this design is a perfect background for the showy mauve peacock feathers, as well as the silk and dried flowers. (FIG. 6-1).

You will need:

- ☐ One 15-inch (38 cm) natural willow wreath
- ☐ Four mauve peacock feathers, each 1 yard (.9 m) long
- ☐ Two stems eggshell silk lilies, each stem containing six flowers with 2-inch (5 cm) heads and two buds
- ☐ Two stems peach silk azaleas, each stem containing six flowers with 2-inch (5 cm) heads
- ☐ Fourteen 3-inch (7.5 cm) white feathers
- ☐ 2-ounce package dried lamb's ear
- ☐ 3-inch (7.5 cm) × 2-inch (5 cm) × 1-inch (2.5 cm) block of Sahara II foam
- ☐ 1-ounce package Spanish moss
- ☐ Two white chenille stems
- ☐ Green floral tape
- ☐ 20-gauge stem wire

Continued

☐ Hot glue gun and sticks

☐ 20-gauge cloth-covered wire

☐ U-shaped craft pins

Fig. 6-1
The soft romantic feeling of peacock feathers and lamb's ear make this a lovely wreath to view.

1. Insert peacock feathers through wreath at an angle near the bottom right side of the wreath. Secure these feathers with glue and small pieces of cloth-covered wire wrapped around the wreath and the feather.

2. Glue the Sahara II foam on the lower left side of the wreath over the location where the feathers are inserted. Secure the foam to the wreath with lengths of chenille stem. Cover the foam with moss and secure the moss in place with craft pins.

3. Individually cut the azaleas away from their main stem so that they each have a 3-inch (7.5 cm) stem. Floral-tape one azalea to a 7-inch (17.5 cm) length of stem wire and insert into the top of the foam at the same angle as the peacock feathers. Floral-tape the remaining stems to 4-inch (10 cm) lengths of stem wire. Insert five around the outside

edge of the foam. Including the first stem previously inserted, a total of six stems should be equally spaced around. Cluster the remaining four flowers randomly into the top of the foam to round out the look.

4. Cut one cluster of three lilies and a bud from the main stem so it has a stem length of 7 inches (17.5 cm). Insert it into the top edge of the foam at the same angle as the feathers, located about 2 inches (5 cm) away from the azalea.

5. Cut remaining lilies and bud individually to 3-inch (7.5 cm) stem lengths. Floral-tape each to 4-inch (10 cm) lengths of stem wire. Insert these randomly among the azaleas to further fill the design.

6. Cut one 10-inch (25.5 cm) stem of lamb's ear and insert at the same angle as the feathers between the tallest lily and azalea. Break the remaining pieces of lamb's ear into approximately 10 pieces ranging in length from 4 inches (10 cm) to 6 inches (15 cm). Insert these randomly through the lilies and azaleas to further fill space.

7. Insert the white feathers into any remaining locations around the design for a nice full look.

POTPOURRI LACE WREATH

This lovely aromatic wreath uses tulle and satin roses for a soft, lush look (FIG. 6-2).

Fig. 6-2
Sacks of potpourri not only give this wreath aroma, but look lovely as well.

You will need:

☐ One 12-inch (30.5 cm) straw wreath

☐ 6¹/₂ yards (6 m) of 1¹/₂-inch-wide (4 cm) lacedge mauve moiré ribbon

☐ 1 yard (.9 m) of 2¹/₂-inch-wide (6.5 cm) eggshell gathered lace

☐ 9 yards (8.1 m) of ⁷/₈-inch-wide (2 cm) French blue lacedge ribbon

☐ 9 yards (8.1 m) of ⁷/₈-inch-wide (2 cm) mauve lacedge ribbon

☐ 7 yards (6.3 m) of 6-inch-wide (15 cm) eggshell tulle

☐ 7 yards (6.3 m) of ¹/₄-inch-wide (.6 cm) French blue picot ribbon

☐ Three stems mauve satin roses, each stem containing four 2-inch (5 cm) rose heads

☐ Thirty-six 3-inch (7.5 cm) wired pearl stems

☐ 6-ounce bag of Victorian Rose potpourri

☐ Cloth-covered wire

☐ Straight pins or corsage pins

☐ Hot glue gun and sticks

Fig. 6-3
A potpourri wall wreath can also be a table centerpiece.

1. Wrap the wreath with the 1¹/₂-inch (4 cm) mauve lacedge ribbon, pinning the ends to secure. Pin the gathered lace around the back of the wreath.

2. Following instructions in chapter 2 and using the ⁷/₈-inch-wide blue ribbon and the ⁷/₈-inch-wide mauve ribbon, make nine four-loop bows of each color, securing each with a length of cloth-covered wire. Pin both colors of bows equally spaced around the wreath on the top and sides. Cut the stems of the pearls to ¹/₄ inch (1.4 cm) and glue two inside each bow.

3. Using the potpourri and tulle and following the directions in chapter 2, form thirty potpourri sacks, tying each with the picot ribbon. Pin and glue the potpourri sacks equally spaced around and through the bows on the wreath.

4. Cut the stems of the satin roses to lengths of 2 to 3 inches (5 cm to 7.5 cm) and glue throughout the ribbon and potpourri sacks equally spaced around the wreath.

CANDLE CENTERPIECE VARIATION

A variation of the Potpourri Lace Wreath described above is to lie it flat on the table and place a hurricane globe and candle in the center. In our example in FIG. 6-3, we have eliminated the silk roses, but all the other materials and techniques described are the same.

RIBBON & LACE HEART WREATH

A simple technique is used to create ribbon poufs which entirely fill the wreath in FIG. 6-4. Various accents can be added to highlight the wreath.
   You will need:

☐ One 22-inch (56 cm) Styrofoam heart form

☐ 25 yards (22.1 m) of 2¹/₂-inch-wide (6.5 cm) lacedge peach ribbon

☐ 12 yards (10.8 m) of ¹/₄-inch-wide (1.3 cm) peach satin ribbon

☐ One stem of peach blossom flowers containing thirty-two 1-inch (2.5 cm) flowers

☐ Twenty-five peach chenille stems

☐ One-hundred 1-inch (2.5 cm) straight pins

☐ 20-gauge cloth-covered wire

Fig. 6-4
Loops and loops of romantic lacedge ribbon create a dazzling wreath.

1. Cut the chenille stems into 3-inch (7.5 cm) lengths and the 2¹/₂-inch (6.5 cm) ribbon into 10-inch (25.5 cm) lengths. Fold one length of the ribbon in half with the wrong sides together lengthwise and cut from the end of the selvage edge to the fold upward at a 45-degree angle. This makes an inverted V at the ribbon edges. Continue with all the pieces of ribbon.

2. Fold one of the ribbon pieces in half with wrong sides together, matching the ends. Pinch the ribbon loop into a gather at its center. Wrap one of the chenille stems around the gathers and twist it tightly all the way to the ends of the length of the chenille. Separate the two

ribbon tails, twisting one piece over so you can see the right side of each tail.

3. Insert the ends of the chenille stem into the foam wreath at the point of the heart. Push a pin from inside the loop through the ribbon and into the foam wreath. This holds the loop in place and hides the chenille stem.

4. Continue this method of forming a loop as directed, inserting and pinning it into the wreath all around the outside. Place each ribbon loop so its edges touch, but don't overlap. You will be forming three rows of loops: one will be around the outside edge, the second will be around the inside edge, and the third will go around the top of the wreath.

5. Cut the flower heads from the main stem so each has a 3-inch (7.5 cm) stem, and glue in clusters randomly around the wreath. Following the instructions in chapter 2 for the basic bow, form several bows using 1 yard (.9 m) of peach satin ribbon for each bow. Glue the bows between the ribbon loops and flowers on the wreath.

OVAL VICTORIAN WREATH

The technique for creating an oval wreath from a circular one is simple and certainly eye-catching, as shown in FIG. 6-5. Victorian styling is complete with the addition of laces, pearls, and roses.

You will need:

☐ One 14-inch (35 cm) straw wreath

☐ 8 yards (7.2 m) of 1¹/₂-inch-wide (4 cm) eggshell moiré ribbon

☐ 9 yards (8.1 m) of 1¹/₂-inch-wide (4 cm) peach lace ribbon

☐ 1²/₃ yards (1.5 m) of 4-inch-wide (10 cm) eggshell lace ribbon

☐ 1 yard (.9 m) of peach satin cording

☐ 6 yards (5.4 m) of ⁵/₈-inch-wide (1.5 cm) celadon green lacedge ribbon

☐ 5 yards (4.5 m) of ⁵/₈-inch-wide (1.5 cm) eggshell lace ribbon

☐ Twelve peach satin roses with 3-inch-wide (7.5 cm) heads

☐ Twelve 3-inch (7.5 cm) pearl sprays

☐ Twelve 4-inch-long (10 cm) celadon green feathers

☐ ¹/₂ yard (.5 m) of 4mm fused pearls

Fig. 6-5
Lace fans, pearls, and ribbon form an eye-catching diagonal design.

☐ ¹/₂ yard (.5 m) of 4mm fused pearls

☐ 28-gauge cloth-covered wire

☐ Hot glue gun and sticks

☐ Straight pins

1. Grab sides of the wreath and push into an oval shape. Cut the 4-inch-wide (10 cm) eggshell lace ribbon into five 12-inch (30.5 cm) lengths. Follow the instructions in chapter 2 to accordion-pleat the ribbon into five lace fans, securing each with a 3-inch (7.5 cm) length of cloth-covered wire.

2. Completely wrap the straw wreath with the eggshell moiré ribbon, securing the ends with straight pins. Follow the instructions in chapter 2 to create the twisted-ribbon technique on the wreath using the peach lace ribbon.

3. Pin and glue three of the lace fans in a semicircle left of center at the top of the wreath. Pin and glue two lace fans to the right of center at the bottom of the wreath with the ends facing each other.

4. Use 12 inches (30.5 cm) each of ⁵/₈ inch (1.5 cm) celadon green lacedge ribbon, ⁵/₈ inch (1.5 m) eggshell lace ribbon, peach satin cording, and fused pearls, pinning one end of each under the top set of fans. Drape these materials across the wreath and pin and glue under the lower set of fans.

5. Following the instructions in chapter 2, you will be forming several basic bows and attaching in the center of the fan clusters. First form a ten-loop bow with 2-inch (5 cm) loops and no center loop, and attach into the center of the top group of fans with the green lacedge ribbon. Using the same ribbon, form an eight-loop bow with 2-inch (5 cm) loops and no center loop, and attach in the center of the lower fans.

6. With the ⁵/₈-inch-wide (1.5 cm) eggshell lace ribbon, form an eight-loop bow with 2-inch (5 cm) loops and no center loop. Attach into the center of the top bow. Repeat with a second bow and attach on top of the lower bow.

7. Using the green lacedge ribbon, form one bow having eight 1¹/₂-inch (4 cm) loops and attach into the center of the top bow. Repeat, forming a second bow, which is attached on top of the lower cluster of bows.

8. Cut the stems of the roses to 1 inch (2.5 cm), and glue six into the top ribbon cluster and four into the lower ribbon cluster. Cut the stems of the pearl stems to ¹/₂ inch (1.3 cm) and glue throughout both bows. Glue the feathers into any remaining open areas.

SPANISH MOSS & DRIED ROSE WREATH

Although the Spanish moss wreath in FIG. 6-6 was purchased as is, you may also purchase a heart-shaped straw wreath and cover it with Spanish moss, pinning in place with U-shaped craft pins.

Fig. 6-6
The romantic dried roses add a lovely feminine touch to the heart-shaped Spanish moss wreath.

You will need:

☐ One 12-inch (30.5 cm) Spanish moss heart-shaped wreath

☐ Sixteen dried rosebuds with heads measuring 1¹/₂ inch (4 cm) in length

☐ 1-ounce package preserved gypsophila

☐ 3 yards (2.7 m) of 1-inch-wide (2.5 cm) floral print ribbon

☐ 4 yards (3.6 m) of ¹/₂-inch-wide (1.3 m) contrasting color moiré ribbon

☐ U-shaped craft pins

☐ Hot glue gun and sticks

☐ Wired wooden picks

☐ 28-gauge cloth-covered wire

1. Following the instructions in chapter 2, form four 6-inch (15 cm) loops of ribbon with the floral print ribbon and eight 6-inch (15 cm) loops from the contrasting moiré ribbon. With the remaining moiré ribbon,

form a ten-loop bow with 2-inch (5 cm) loops, 8-inch (20 cm) streamers, and no center loop. Attach this bow to the top center of the wreath. With the remaining floral print ribbon, form a bow having 2-inch (5 cm) loops and 8-inch (20 cm) streamers, and attach over the moiré bow. Bring the streamers of both ribbons to the sides of the wreath and pin in place.

2. Form small bunches of the gypsophila and pin and glue around the top portion of the wreath. Insert the ribbon loops randomly throughout the design. Glue the rosebuds between the ribbon and gypsophila.

GATHERED LACE WREATH

Simple to create and beautiful to view, this wreath is a great gift item as well as a perfect addition for your own home (FIG. 6-7).

You will need:

- [ ] One 16-inch (40.5 cm) straw wreath
- [ ] 8 yards (7.2 m) of 1¹/2-inch-wide (4 cm) peach ribbon
- [ ] 1¹/2 yards (1.3 m) of 5-inch-wide (12.5 cm) eggshell gathered lace
- [ ] 3 yards (2.7 m) of 4mm fused pearls
- [ ] 3 yards (2.7 m) of peach satin cording
- [ ] 3 yards (2.7 m) of eggshell velvet tubing
- [ ] 2 yards (1.8 m) of 3-inch-wide (7.5 cm) peach ribbon
- [ ] Hot glue gun and sticks
- [ ] Straight pins
- [ ] 28-gauge cloth-covered wire

Fig. 6-7
The Gathered Lace Wreath is simple to create and lovely to look at.

1. Completely wrap wreath with the 1¹/2-inch-wide (4 cm) peach satin ribbon, pinning ends to secure. Pin the gathered lace around the top side of the wreath in the center.

2. Following the instructions in chapter 2, braid the fused pearls, peach cording, and velvet tubing together, securing the ends with 2-inch (5 cm) lengths of cloth-covered wire. Pin and glue the braid over the center of the gathered lace on top of the pins, which secure the lace to the wreath.

3. Using the 3-inch-wide (7.5 cm) peach ribbon and following the instructions in chapter 2, form a tailored bow. Attach to the top of the wreath with pins, slightly to the left side of the wreath.

PLEATED RIBBON WREATH

The beauty of this wreath lies in the layered rows of pleated ribbon. The rows alternate in ribbon types for contrast and texture changes (FIG. 6-8).

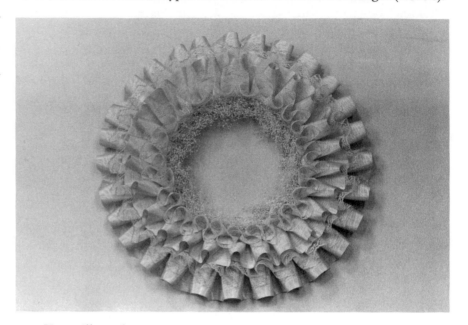

You will need:

- [ ] One 12-inch (30.5 cm) flat or half-round Styrofoam wreath form
- [ ] 6¹/₂ yards (6 m) of 3-inch-wide (7.5 cm) peach moiré ribbon
- [ ] 6 yards (5.4 cm) of 3-inch-wide (7.5 cm) peach lacedge ribbon
- [ ] 1-ounce package preserved baby's breath
- [ ] Hot glue gun and sticks
- [ ] Straight pins
- [ ] Stapler and staples
- [ ] Optional: Bow using 2 yards (1.8 m) each of ¹/₂-inch-wide (1.3 cm) peach satin ribbon and eggshell lace ribbon.

1. Box-pleat 4 yards (3.6 m) of peach moiré following the diagrams in FIG. 6-9. Use the stapler to secure the pleats as you go. Pin this ribbon to the center top of the wreath, all the way around.

2. Repeat the box-pleating process with 3¹/₂ yards (3.2 m) of lacedge ribbon. Pin this row of lace approximately ¹/₂ inch (1.3 cm) in closer to the center of the wreath.

3. Using 2¹/₂ yards (2.3 m) of peach moiré ribbon, repeat the above process, and pin this row of lace a little less than ¹/₂ inch (1.3 m) closer to the center of the wreath. Use the remaining 2¹/₂ yards (2.3 m) of lacedge ribbon, repeat the folding process, and pin this row around the inside of the wreath.

4. Form clusters of baby's breath approximately 3 inches (7.5 cm) long and glue these clusters around the inside of the wreath.

5. If desired, attach the bow in the center bottom of the design.

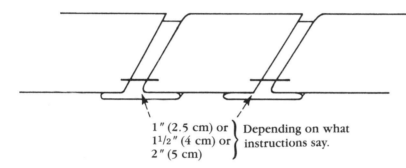

1 ″ (2.5 cm) or ⎫
1¹/₂ ″ (4 cm) or ⎬ Depending on what instructions say.
2 ″ (5 cm) ⎭

Fig. 6-9
Follow this diagram when box-pleating ribbon.

SHIRRED VICTORIAN RIBBON & ROSES WREATH

The lush look of Victorian styling is evident in this wreath (FIG. 6-10), with the embellished look of roses, ivy, and feathers.

You will need:

☐ One 14-inch (35 cm) straw wreath

☐ 8 yards (7.2 m) of 1¹/₂-inch-wide (4 cm) mauve moiré ribbon

☐ 4 yards (3.6 m) of 8-inch-wide (20 cm) eggshell lace or lace fabric

☐ Four mauve china silk rosebuds with 2-inch (5 cm) heads

☐ Two mauve china silk open roses with 3-inch (7.5 cm) heads

☐ Two stems French blue satin lilies, each stem containing two 5-inch (12.5 cm) open flowers and one 3-inch (7.5 cm) lily bud

☐ Fourteen 2-inch (5 cm) English ivy leaves

☐ Twelve 6-inch (15 cm) ivory plumes (feathers)

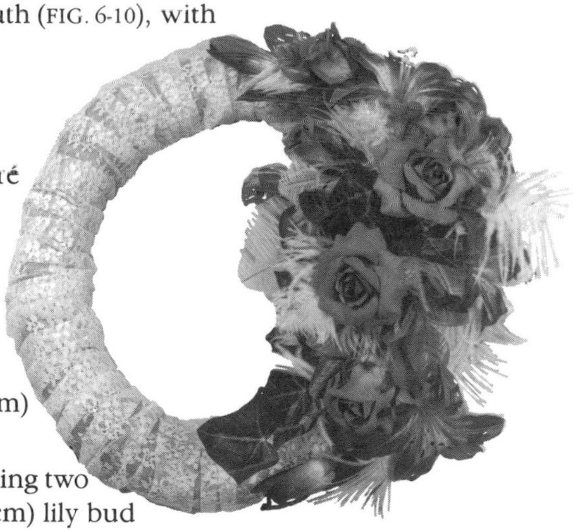

Fig. 6-10
The embellished look of this wreath helps create a Victorian mood.

Continued

☐ Straight pins

☐ 3-inch (7.5 cm) block Sahara II foam

☐ ¹/₂ ounce Spanish moss

☐ U-shaped craft pins

☐ Hot glue gun and sticks

1. Completely wrap the wreath with the mauve moiré ribbon. Following the instructions in chapter 2, shir the 8-inch (20 cm) lace over the moiré ribbon on the wreath.

2. Hot glue the Sahara II foam to the right center of the wreath. Cover the foam with moss and secure with craft pins. Cut the lily buds from the main stem so that they have 6-inch (15 cm) stem lengths. Curve the stems and insert one into each end of the foam so that the stems follow the curve of the wreath.

3. Cut the stems of the rosebuds so that they have 4-inch (10 cm) stem lengths. Gently curve the stems and insert one into each end of the wreath so that they fall in line with the lily already placed.

4. Cut the stem of one open rose to a stem length of 3 inches (7.5 cm) and insert into the center of the foam. Cut the stems of the remaining roses to 3 inches and insert around the main rose in the center of the design.

5. Cut two of the open lilies to stem lengths of 4 inches (10 cm) and two roses to stem lengths of 3 inches (7.5 cm). Insert the two shorter stems in open spaces near the center rose and the two longer roses a little further away in line with the outer flowers. This whole grouping should form a nice full crescent shape.

6. Insert the feathers and ivy leaves throughout the design to fill space and add color and contrast between the roses and lilies.

CHAPTER 7

Masculine Wreaths

Creating wreaths for the men in our lives is often a challenge to our creative abilities. Most florals and floral-related products have a feminine connotation, and men find them inappropriate when hung in rooms where they spend most of their time.

This chapter contains several wreaths that have a rich, masculine feel. Try to pull colors from the wallpaper of the room where the wreath is to be hung so that it enhances the room.

NATURALS CRESCENT WREATH

The rich look of grapevine is well accented in the use of the bronze palms. Eucalyptus gives a much-needed texture and color change (FIG. 7-1).

You will need:

- [ ] One 18-inch (45.5 cm) grapevine wreath
- [ ] Eight 6-inch (15 cm) to 8-inch (20 cm) burnt bronze palm stems
- [ ] 4 yards (3.6 m) of 3-inch-wide (7.5 cm) eggshell mesh ribbon
- [ ] Four 3-inch (7.5 cm) lotus pods on picks
- [ ] Five 3-inch (7.5 cm) natural cardone puffs on picks
- [ ] 1/4 pound green baby eucalyptus
- [ ] 3-ounce bundle orange campo flowers
- [ ] Wired wooden picks
- [ ] Two eggshell chenille stems
- [ ] Hot glue gun and sticks
- [ ] Optional: Spray the grapevine wreath with glossy wood tone from Design Master to give it a luster and shine.

Fig. 7-1
Rustic dried materials and pods form a striking crescent design.

1. Cut the stems of two bronze palm stems to 1-inch (2.5 cm) lengths. Glue facing in opposite directions so palm cuts wreath in half, as shown in FIG. 7-2. Cut two more palm stems and insert next to the first ones as shown in FIG. 7-3. Cut four more palm stems and group in the center of the design, with two palm facing in each direction.

Fig. 7-2 (Left)
The first two palm stems are placed so that they cut the wreath in half.

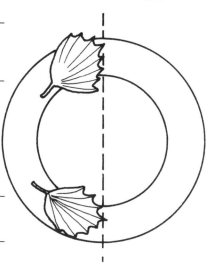

Fig. 7-3 (Right)
The second two palms reinforce the crescent line.

2. Following instructions in chapter 2, form a bow having eight 6-inch (15 cm) loops and no streamers. Secure the bow in the center between the palm. Cut two 18-inch (45.5 cm) lengths of ribbon. Secure one end of each with one-half chenille stem. Glue one chenille stem end under the center palm on each side of the bow. Swag the streamers up through the palm, securing along the way.

3. Insert one pod above and one below the bow. Insert the third pod above the top pod angled around the wreath. Break off the stem on the fourth pod and glue it into the center of the bow.

4. One cardone puff should be inserted on top of the lowest palm and ribbon streamer. Insert the second above the first and next to the lotus pod. Insert the third cardone puff below and to the left of the center lotus pod, and the fourth above and to the right of the same pod. Place the last puff above and to the left of the fourth puff.

5. Cut six stems of eucalyptus to lengths of 10 inches (25.5 cm). Insert three into the upper portion and three into the lower portion around the outside palms. Break the remaining eucalyptus into twelve 6-inch (15 cm) pieces and glue them randomly throughout.

6. Break the campo flowers into 8-inch (20 cm) lengths and secure a quarter-size bunch to a wood pick as described in chapter 1. Prepare eight and insert throughout the design.

FEATHERED WILLOW WREATH

The dramatic diagonal line evident in this design effectively moves the eye of the viewer so that he sees and appreciates the whole wreath (FIG. 7-4). The feathers are very masculine in nature and would be a perfect accent for the man who loves hunting.

You will need:

☐ One 14-inch (35 cm) bleached willow wreath

☐ 1-ounce package ming moss

☐ Two blue pheasant feathers approximately 1 yard (.9 m) long

☐ Three natural peacock feathers approximately 1 yard (.9 m) long

☐ Two bleached yanagimaki

☐ 1 yard of 1½-inch-wide (4 cm) eggshell mesh ribbon

☐ 1½ yards (1.3 m) of ⅞-inch-wide (2 cm) blue mesh ribbon

☐ 1-ounce package natural preserved galaxy gypsophila

☐ Eight assorted cones and pods approximately 1½ inches (4 cm) long

☐ Hot glue gun and glue sticks

☐ One eggshell chenille stem

Fig. 7-4
The feathers used in this design make it a perfect gift for the woodsman in your family.

1. Begin by glueing the moss to the lower left corner of the wreath. Cut two pheasant feathers 18 inches (45.5 cm) measuring from the feather tip. Glue these two into the moss angled up to the right. Cut two 12 inch (30.5 cm) lengths of the same feathers, measuring from the end. Glue these two into the bottom of the moss, angled away from the wreath to the left.

2. Cut 12-inch (30.5 cm) lengths of peacock feathers starting at the tips of the feathers. Glue three into the moss, angled up to the right around the pheasant feathers. Cut 10-inch (25.5 cm) lengths of peacock feathers starting at the feather end. Glue these into the moss, angled to the lower left, in front of the pheasant feather ends.

3. Cut a 10-inch (25.5 cm) length of yanagimaki, measuring from the tip of the stem. Glue into the foam angled to the lower right. Cut 10 inches (25.5 cm) of the same yanagimaki, measuring from the other end. Glue this stem into the moss, angled to the upper left. This should resemble a plus sign with the feathers. Repeat these steps with the other yanagimaki, but cutting the stem length to 8 inches (20 cm).

4. Form a bow with two 5-inch (12.5 cm) and two 10-inch (25.5 cm) streamers using the eggshell ribbon. With the blue ribbon, form a tailored bow having two 2-inch (5 cm) loops, two 3-inch (7.5 cm) loops, and 10-inch (25.5 cm) streamers. Following the instructions in chapter 2, form a layered bow with these two bows, placing the blue bow on

top of the eggshell one. Wire this bow over the moss at the location the feathers are inserted.

5. Break the gypsophila into 3-inch (7.5 cm) to 6-inch (15 cm) pieces. Glue them into the wreath, following the line of the yanagimaki. Break the stems of the pods to 1 inch (2.5 cm), and glue around and through the bow loops and dried materials.

NATURALS WREATH

The rich beautiful tones of nature come through on this design. Since many of the materials are similar, their vivid colors allow them to stand apart from each other (FIG. 7-5).

Fig. 7-5
This wreath is accented with the use of many colors and textures of pods and dried materials.

You will need:

☐ One 14-inch (35 cm) sphagnum moss wreath

☐ 2-ounce package German statice

☐ 2-ounce package candy tuff

☐ Ten assorted large pods, each measuring approximately 4 inches (10 cm)

☐ 1-ounce package peach-colored berries

☐ Eight begun fruit (type of pod)

☐ Six straw flowers

☐ Twenty mini pinecones

Continued

☐ Five plumosum cones 2½ inches (6.5 cm) wide

☐ Four flat floral pods approximately 2 inches (5 cm) wide

☐ 1 ounce white statice sinuata

☐ Six mini lotus pods

☐ Five assorted mini pods of your choice

☐ Three Mexican hat pods

☐ Hot glue gun and sticks

Note: The varieties and types of pods used in this design can easily be changed, if the exact pods are unavailable in your area. Choose a wide selection of looks, textures, and colors and you will surely have a beautiful design!

1. The sphagnum moss wreath may have moss on only one side and have the straw showing through on the other. If this is the case, turn the wreath over with the moss side down and work on glueing the items to the straw side.

2. Divide the wreath into five sections and glue a cluster of German statice across the wreath from inside to outside at each of the five locations. Glue a cluster of candy tuff in between each statice cluster.

3. Glue one larger pod on either side of statice in various locations on the wreath. Glue the remaining materials throughout the wreath to cover. Attach the materials in clumps or groups around the wreath to create the best impact of color and material.

NATURALS CENTERPIECE

A look of continuity prevails when a second wreath is made exactly as described above, but placed on a table with a hurricane globe and 3-inch (7.5 cm) candle in the center of the globe.

BABY'S BREATH & POD WREATH

The difference of color shown in the filler materials used in this design are especially eye-catching. Other colors of gypsophila could also be combined for a more versatile color scheme (FIG. 7-6).

You will need:

☐ One 14-inch (35 cm) straw wreath

☐ Two 6-ounce packages of orange gypsophila

☐ One 6-ounce package of natural preserved baby's breath

☐ Eight large flat pods approximately 3 inches (7.5 cm) across

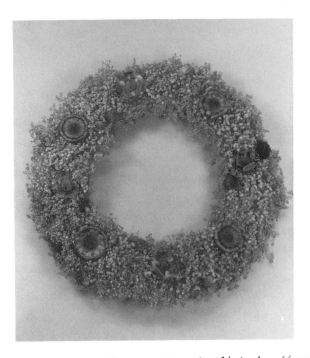

Fig. 7-6
The striking colors used in this wreath create the contrast necessary to make it spectacular.

☐ Ten small pods approximately 1½ inches (4 cm) across

☐ Hot glue gun and sticks

☐ U-shaped craft pins

1. Break off 2-inch (5 cm) clusters of the orange gypsophila. Place a craft pin over the ends and pin into the straw wreath. Pin clusters side-by-side across the wreath. Pin the next row of clusters over the ends of the row before. Continue in this fashion all the way around the outside and inside of the wreath. Leave the top center of the wreath bare.

2. Repeat by making clusters with the baby's breath and filling in the area on top of the wreath. These materials can either be facing the opposite direction or everything can be facing the same direction.

3. Break off the stems on the pods and glue them equally spaced around the top of the wreath.

EUCALYPTUS CRESCENT WREATH

The crescent design on this wreath creates an interesting dimension when placed over the eucalyptus base (FIG. 7-7).

   You will need:

☐ One 16-inch (40.5 cm) straw wreath

☐ 1½ pounds baby brown eucalyptus

Continued

Fig. 7-7
The beauty of this eucalyptus wreath is accented by a lovely crescent design of pods and ribbon.

☐ Twelve assorted pods with heads measuring 2 inches (5 cm) to 4 inches (10 cm)

☐ 1¹/₂ yards (1.3 m) of 1¹/₂-inch-wide (4 cm) plaid ribbon

☐ 1-ounce package preserved baby's breath

☐ One eggshell chenille stem

☐ ¹/₂ pound U-shaped craft pins

☐ Hot glue gun and sticks

1. Break off clusters of three to four eucalyptus stems measuring 3 inches (7.5 cm) in length. Holding the cluster together, place a craft pin over the ends of the cluster and insert into the wreath to secure the cluster to the wreath. Continue forming clusters and placing them side-by-side around the wreath. Move down the wreath in rows, making sure the heads of one row cover the ends of the row above it.

2. Following instructions in chapter 2, form a basic bow with eight 2¹/₂-inch (6.5 cm) loops and two 10-inch (25.5 cm) streamers. Pin and glue this bow to the left side of the wreath in the center.

3. Break pieces of baby's breath to a length of 4 inches (10 cm) and glue them to form a crescent shape on the left side of the wreath. Cut all the pod stems to 3 inch (7.5 cm) lengths and glue randomly throughout the crescent of baby's breath.

COUNTRY FLAT WALL BASKET

The rich, deep colors of this basket suggest a masculine feeling (FIG. 7- 8).

Fig. 7-8
A flat wall basket adds a
touch of deep rich color.

You will need:

☐ One 12-inch-tall (30.5 cm) × 9-inch-wide (22.5 cm) flat wall basket
☐ 1-ounce package preserved gypsophila
☐ One stem orange berries with fourteen 1/2-inch (1.3 cm) berries
☐ 1 1/2 yard (1.3 m) of 1-inch-wide (2.5 cm) rust plaid ribbon
☐ 1 yard (.9 m) of 1-inch-wide (2.5 cm) orange mesh ribbon
☐ Eight 1-inch (2.5 cm) rust starburst flowers
☐ Two eggshell chenille stems
☐ Hot glue gun and sticks

1. Break clusters of preserved gypsophila to 2 inch (5 cm) lengths, and glue bunches around basket handle and along top edge of basket. Glue berries in clusters of two and three berries per cluster.

2. Cut the stems of the starburst flowers to 1 inch (2.5 cm) and glue around the baby's breath on the basket. Form a layered bow following the instructions in chapter 2. The bottom bow is the rust plaid ribbon

and should have eight 2½-inch (6.5 cm) loops and 6-inch (15 cm) streamers. The top bow is made with eight 2-inch (5 cm) loops and 6-inch (15 cm) streamers. Secure the bows with the chenille stems, then attach the bows to the left side of the basket where the handle and basket meet.

CRESCENT WALL PLAQUE

Wallpieces can be created with the use of interesting slices of wood plaques. The ones used here are walnut slices. Try to choose slices with interesting grain (FIG. 7-9).

You will need:

- [ ] One walnut slice plaque, 14 inches (35 cm) × 9 inches (22.5 cm)
- [ ] Six stems French blue mums, each stem containing one 3-inch (7.5 cm) flower
- [ ] Two stems eggshell lilies, each stem containing three 2-inch (5 cm) flowers and one bud
- [ ] One stem slate blue double blossom flowers with six clusters of four 1-inch (2.5 cm) flowers
- [ ] Twenty-four pieces of 3-inch (7.5 cm) silk Boston fern stems
- [ ] 2 yards (1.8 m) of 1-inch-wide (2.5 cm) eggshell mesh ribbon
- [ ] Five pencil cattails
- [ ] 3-inch (7.5 cm) block Sahara II foam
- [ ] 1-ounce package Spanish moss
- [ ] ¼-pound package baby green eucalyptus
- [ ] U-shaped craft pins
- [ ] Wired wooden picks
- [ ] Hot glue gun and sticks
- [ ] Green floral tape
- [ ] 20-gauge stem wire
- [ ] Sawtooth hanger

Fig. 7-9
Walnut plaques make beautiful bases for wallpiece designs.

1. Glue the foam to the left side of the plaque, cover with moss, and secure moss with craft pins. Cut a 12-inch (30.5 cm) and a 10-inch (25.5 cm) length of eucalyptus and insert into the top of the foam. Cut a 9-inch (22.5 cm) and an 8-inch (20 cm) piece of eucalyptus and insert into the bottom of the foam. Insert 4-inch (10 cm) pieces between the upper and lower eucalyptus along the outside of the foam. These should be placed a few inches apart to visually connect the upper and lower stems.

2. Cut two mum stems to 6 inches (15 cm) and insert one in the top of the foam and one in the bottom on top of the eucalyptus. Cut the remaining stems to 3 inches (7.5 cm) and insert two into a line to visually connect the first two mums. Insert one on either side of this imaginary line.

3. Cut the lilies and buds off of their main stems and floral-tape each to a 3-inch (7.5 cm) length of stem wire. Insert these throughout the design to fill space and add color and texture changes.

4. Following the instructions in chapter 2, form eight ribbon loops, attaching each to a wired wooden pick. Insert these around the design to fill space between flowers. Insert three cattails into the top of the design and two into the bottom of the design, as shown in FIG. 7-8. Cut all the Boston fern stems to 1/2 inches (1.3 cm), gently shape, and insert between the materials in the design to add contrast and fullness. Attach the sawtooth hanger to the back of the plaque for hanging the design.

WALNUT PLAQUE CENTERPIECE

The design in FIG. 7-10 is a lying-down version of the Crescent Wall Plaque above. To add a little contrast and color change, we replaced the mums with a zinnia-like flower and added twelve mini pinecones on 2-inch (5 cm) stems to the flowers in the design. The candles are inserted into wooden candle cups glued to the plaque. We used an 8-inch (20 cm), 10-inch (25.5 cm), and 12-inch (30.5 cm) candle.

CONTEMPORARY
LEAF & POD WREATH

This design is especially unique in the treatment used to cover the foam wreath. The preserved salal leaves gives this design an exceptional outdoor look and feel (FIG. 7-11).

You will need:

☐ One 14-inch (35 cm) Styrofoam wreath

☐ One package preserved salal leaves with approximately fifty 3-inch (7.5 cm) leaves per package

☐ Six white wood flowers, each with 3-inch-wide (7.5 cm) head

☐ 1-ounce package purple statice sinuata

Continued

Fig. 7-10
The same idea of using a walnut plaque is recreated into a candle tablepiece.

☐ Three white banana leaf pods, each 9 inches (22.5 cm) to 12 inches (30.5 cm) in length

☐ 3 yards (2.7 m) of 1-inch-wide (2.5 cm) celadon green mesh ribbon

☐ Three whitewashed cycas rib

☐ 3-inch (7.5 cm) block Sahara II

☐ 1-ounce package Spanish moss

☐ 1 inch (2.5 cm) straight pins

☐ White craft glue

☐ U-shaped craft pins

☐ One eggshell chenille stem

1. Pick all the leaves off of the stems and pin individually to the wreath. Overlap the leaves side-by-side around the wreath, from the inside to the outside. New rows should cover the ends of the rows before. Since bare wire tends to pull away from foam, dip each pin into glue before inserting into the foam wreath.

Fig. 7-11
Preserved salal leaves give an interesting background for this wreath design.

2. Glue the foam block to the lower left area of the wreath. Cover the foam with Spanish moss and secure the moss with U-shaped craft pins. Cut the center cycas rib to a length of 20 inches (50.5 cm) and insert it into the foam, angled slightly to the right. Cut the other two cycas ribs to lengths of 16 inches (40.5 cm) and insert one on either side of the first one.

3. Cut the banana leaf pod stems to 12 inches (30.5 cm), 10 inches (25.5 cm), and 7 inches (17.5 cm). Insert into the foam as shown in FIG. 7-11.

4. Form a bow with the ribbon following the instructions in chapter 2. The bow should have several 4-inch (10 cm) loops and be secured with the chenille stem. Pin the bow to the left side of the foam.

5. Cut the stems of the wood flowers to 3-inch (7.5 cm) and 4-inch (10 cm) lengths and insert into a cluster as shown in the photo.

6. The statice should be broken into shorter pieces and inserted around and through the other featured materials. One stem of statice extends up the center of the design, a little shorter than the tallest pod.

LIGHT & AIRY GRAPEVINE WREATH

The soft, open nature of the materials used to construct this wreath give it a very open, airy appearance. It is the perfect addition to a room that is not extremely heavy in decor (FIG. 7-12).

You will need:

☐ One 15-inch (38 cm) grapevine wreath

☐ 3 yards (2.7 m) of 3-inch-wide (7.5 cm) celadon green mesh ribbon

☐ 2-ounce package preserved galaxy gypsophila

☐ 1-ounce package celadon green lagurus (bunny tails)

☐ 1 ounce package teal lagurus

☐ One chenille stem

☐ Hot glue gun and sticks

1. Following the instructions in chapter 2, form a tailored bow using the mesh ribbon. Allow the streamers to swag down the front of the wreath, as shown in the photo. Glue these ends to the front of the wreath.

2. Break the galaxy gypsophila into 4-inch (10 cm) pieces and glue it around the wreath and between the loops of the bow. Keep it light and airy in appearance. Break the lagurus stems to lengths of 3 inches (7.5 cm) and 4 inches (10 cm), and glue into the gypsophila around the wreath and into the bow loops.

Fig. 7-12
This grapevine wreath has a soft, delicate appearance because of the airy way the materials were attached.

Special Occasions

There are times in our lives when we want to create something extra special for someone dear to us. This chapter is full of ideas for those special times in our lives.

PORTRAIT CAMEO WREATH

This wreath is a perfect gift for moms, grandmothers, or family far away. Each tiny cameo spotlights a different member of the family (FIG. 8-1).

To complete each single cameo, you will need:

☐ One 3-inch (7.5 cm) oval of foam-centered board or cardboard

☐ 12-inch (30.5 cm) lengths of three different colors of 1/4-inch-wide (.6 cm) picot ribbon

☐ 1 yard (.9 m) of 2 mm fused pearls

☐ 12-inch (30.5 cm) length of 2-inch-wide (5 cm) gathered lace

☐ Hot glue gun and sticks

☐ White craft glue

☐ 28-gauge cloth-covered wire

1. Cut the picture to fit the oval cardboard or foam-centered board and glue in place (FIG. 8-2). Following the braiding instructions in chapter 2, braid together the three different colors of picot ribbon, securing the ends with cloth-covered wire. Glue the braid around the outside edge of the board.

2. Glue the gathered lace around the back of the board under the braid. Glue three rows of fused pearls in a row inside of the braid and around the picture.

Fig. 8-1 (Above Left) The Portrait Cameo Wreath can be a very personal gift for a special family member.

Fig. 8-2 (Above Right) The individual cameos can be created and given as gifts by themselves.

To complete the wreath, you will need:

- ☐ Six single cameo pieces. (*Note:* This number may be larger or smaller depending on the number of people you would like to highlight. Always equally space the cameos around. If you use more than six, you may need to use a larger wreath frame and more dried materials.)
- ☐ One 18-inch (45.5 cm) straw wreath
- ☐ Four 4-ounce packages of bleached glittered gypsophila
- ☐ 6 yards (5.4 m) of 1¹/₂-inch-wide (4 cm) pink moiré ribbon
- ☐ 6 yards (5.4 m) of 1¹/₂-inch-wide (4 cm) blue moiré ribbon
- ☐ U-shaped craft pins
- ☐ Hot glue gun and sticks
- ☐ Three blue chenille stems
- ☐ Three pink chenille stems

1. Break off clusters of gypsophila 3 inches (7.5 cm) long. Place a craft pin over the end of the cluster and pin into the wreath securely. Continue to add clusters from the inside to the outside edge of the wreath in a row. After forming the first row, start a second row. The heads of the new row should overlap the ends of the first row. Continue until the entire wreath is covered.

2. Glue the cameos equally spaced around the wreath. With the pink ribbon, form three bows with eight 3-inch (7.5 cm) loops. Form three of the same bows with the blue ribbon. Secure all with chenille stems and pin and glue the bows around the inside and outside of the wreath as shown in FIG. 8-1.

POTPOURRI HEARTS WREATH

Special hearts are created using potpourri and glue as the focal point of this design. The hearts are lovely little items that can also be individually decorated and given as gifts (FIG. 8-3).

You will need:

☐ One 14-inch (35 cm) Styrofoam heart-shaped wreath

☐ 1 pound package rose potpourri

☐ 12 yards (10.8 m) of 1¹/₂-inch (4 cm) pink moiré ribbon

☐ 12 yards (10.8 m) of 1¹/₂-inch (4 cm) white lace ribbon

☐ 2¹/₂ yards (2.3 m) of ¹/₂-inch-wide (1.3 cm) pink moiré ribbon

☐ One 2-inch (5 cm) heart-shaped cookie cutter

☐ One 3-inch (7.5 cm) heart-shaped cookie cutter

☐ One 4-inch (10 cm) heart-shaped cookie cutter

☐ 28-gauge cloth-covered wire

☐ Straight pins

☐ White craft glue

1. Completely wrap the wreath with 9 yards (8.1 m) of the 1¹/₂-inch-wide (4 cm) pink moiré, pinning the ends to secure. Follow the instructions in chapter 2 and using 9 yards (8.1 m) of the white lace ribbon, create the twisted ribbon technique, completely covering the wreath.

2. Mix together 3 parts of potpourri to 1 part of white craft glue in an old or disposable bowl. Lay the cookie cutters onto waxed paper and fill with the potpourri/glue mixture. Push down to completely fill (FIG. 8-4). Wait about 15 minutes, then gently push the molded heart out of the cookie cutter and let dry overnight. Form the following number of potpourri hearts: nine 2-inch (5 cm), one 3-inch (7.5 cm), and one 4-inch (10 cm).

3. Refer to FIG. 8-3 for placement: Glue the 4-inch (10 cm) heart at the upper left corner of the wreath; glue the 3-inch (7.5 cm) heart at center side of wreath; and glue three 2-inch (5 cm) hearts at tip of foam heart as shown.

Fig. 8-3
The Potpourri Hearts Wreath is striking when displayed on a tall wall location.

Fig. 8-4
Potpourri hearts are formed with 3 parts of potpourri and 1 part of glue.

4. Cut the following lengths of the ¹/₂-inch-wide (1.3 cm) pink moiré ribbon: 8-inch (20 cm), 9-inch (22.5 cm), 11-inch (28 cm), 13-inch (33 cm), 16-inch (40.5 cm), and 20-inch (50.5 cm).

5. Glue one end of each ribbon to the top of one 2-inch (5 cm) heart. Hold together all the other ends of the ribbon and pin and glue under the bottom potpourri heart on the foam heart wreath.

6. Following instructions in chapter 2, form a tailored bow with the 2-inch-wide (5 cm) white lace. The bow should have 12-inch (30.5 cm) streamers and a set of 4-inch (10 cm), 3-inch (7.5 cm), and 2-inch (5 cm) loops. Glue the bow on top of the ribbon ends at the base of the wreath.

7. Using the 1¹/₂-inch (4 cm) pink moiré ribbon, form two basic bows with six 2-inch (5 cm) loops. Glue one between the 4-inch (10 cm) and 3-inch (7.5 cm) hearts and one between the 3-inch (7.5 cm) and 2-inch (5 cm) hearts.

WHEAT WREATH

The beautiful textures of wheat make this wreath visually exciting. This would make a wonderful housewarming gift, as wheat is a symbol of good luck and prosperity when displayed in the home (FIG. 8-5).

You will need:

☐ One 12-inch (30.5 cm) straw wreath

☐ Two 1-pound bundles of wheat

☐ 2 yards (1.8 m) of 3-inch-wide (7.5 cm) green plaid ribbon

☐ U-shaped craft pins

Fig. 8-5
Wheat is said to bring good
luck to a household where
it is displayed.

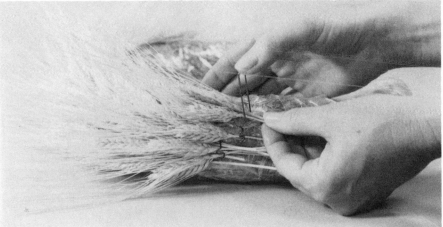

Fig. 8-6
Simply attach clusters of
wheat with U-shaped craft
pins.

☐ One green chenille stem

☐ Hot glue gun and sticks

1. Break off small clusters of wheat containing 4 to 5 pieces. Lay the
   wheat onto the wreath and place a craft pin over the ends and securely
   into the wreath to hold in place (FIG. 8-6). You may wish to add a dab of

glue at the location of the insertion of the pin. Place clusters side-by-side from the outside to the inside edge of the wreath. After completing a row, begin on the next row. The heads of the wheat in the new row should cover the stems of the wheat in the row before. Continue to cover the entire wreath.

2. Form a basic bow with eight 3-inch (7.5 cm) loops and secure to the lower center of the wreath.

"WELCOME BABY" WREATH

Soft pastel colors combined with bleached white gypsophila create a dazzling look, perfect as a gift for the new mom (FIG. 8-7)!

Fig. 8-7
The "Welcome Baby"
Wreath is a lovely gift for a
new mother.

You will need:

☐ One 12-inch (30.5 cm) straw wreath

☐ 6 yards (5.4 m) of 1¹/₂-inch (4 cm) pink moiré ribbon

☐ 8 yards (7.2 m) of 1¹/₂-inch (4 cm) pastel gingham lacedge ribbon

☐ 8 yards (7.2 m) of 1¹/₂-inch (4 cm) lavender striped ribbon

☐ 8 yards (7.2 m) of 1¹/₂-inch (4 cm) pink floral cotton ribbon

☐ 2 yards (1.8 m) of ¹/₂-inch (1.3 cm) lavender picot ribbon

☐ One 4-ounce package glittered bleached gypsophila

☐ Two purple silk rosebuds with 1-inch (2.5 cm) heads

☐ One stem pink double blossoms with six sprigs of four 1-inch (2.5 cm) flowers

☐ One stem lavender starburst flowers with six sections of six flowers each

☐ 28-gauge cloth-covered wire

☐ U-shaped craft pins

☐ Hot glue gun and sticks

1. Completely wrap the wreath with the 1¹/₂-inch (4 cm) pink moiré ribbon, securing the ends with craft pins. Following the instructions in chapter 2, form a layered bow using 2 yards (1.8 m) of the gingham lacedge, the floral cotton ribbon, and the 2 yards (1.8 m) of picot ribbon. Set this bow aside.

2. Form small basic bows using 1 yard (.9 m) each of the remaining ribbon. Pin all the bows randomly around the outside edges of the wreath. Break clusters of the gypsophila into 2-inch (5 cm) clusters and glue around the top center of the wreath to fill.

3. Pin the layered bow to the bottom center of the wreath. Cut the stems of the silk materials to 3-inch (7.5 cm) lengths and glue on either side of the bow.

POPCORN WREATH

Here's another great wreath for a housewarming or perhaps a game-night party—easy to create and fun to look at (FIG. 8-8)!
    You will need:

☐ One 12-inch (30.5 cm) straw wreath

☐ 1 cup popped popcorn (measurement prior to popping)

☐ 5 yards (4.5 m) of ⁵/₈-inch (1.5 cm) red heart patterned ribbon

☐ White craft glue

☐ One chenille stem

1. Spread glue over sections of the straw wreath and press the popped corn over these sections. Continue around the wreath until completely covered.

Fig. 8-8
Popcorn Wreaths are fun to make and give as gifts.

2. After the glue dries, go back and fill in any empty spots individually.

3. When completely dry, attach the bow. The bow is made with eighteen to twenty 3-inch (7.5 cm) loops. Attach extra streamers by wiring them into the back of the bow. Glue the bow to the base of the wreath.

LOOPS & MORE LOOPS WREATH

This design is perfect for a feminine birthday gift, perhaps for an aunt or grandmother (FIG. 8-9).

Fig. 8-9
The soft, delicate look of this untwisted paper wreath will be much appreciated by its recipient.

You will need:

☐ One 8-inch (20 cm) Styrofoam wreath

☐ 9 yards (8.1 m) untwisted eggshell paper ribbon

☐ 1-ounce package mauve painted gypsophila

☐ 1-ounce package blue Florentine (type of dried material)

☐ U-shaped craft pins

☐ 28-gauge cloth-covered wire

☐ Hot glue gun and sticks

☐ White craft glue

1. With the untwisted paper ribbon, form a bow having four 2-inch (5 cm) loops and two 8-inch (20 cm) streamers. Pin and glue this bow to the top of the wreath.

2. Cut the remaining ribbon into 8-inch (20 cm) pieces. Bring the ends of one piece together and pinch to form a loop. Place a craft pin over the pinched ribbon ends. Dip the pin into glue and then into the foam wreath.

3. Continue pinning loops of ribbon around the wreath, overlapping as you go around from side to side. Be sure to completely cover wreath.

4. Break off pieces of gypsophila and Florentine to 3-inch (7.5 cm) lengths and glue throughout the loops in the wreath.

Index